AMERICAN HERITAGE
COOKBOOK

AMERICAN HERITAGE
COOKBOOK

classic regional dishes in 200 step by step recipes

Carla Capalbo & Laura Washburn

HERMES
HOUSE

For Marie, my grandmother,
who has always been my inspiration. Carla

This edition is published by Hermes House, an imprint of Anness Publishing Ltd,
Hermes House, 88–89 Blackfriars Road, London SE1 8HA
tel. 020 7401 2077; fax 020 7633 9499
www.hermeshouse.com; www.annesspublishing.com

If you like the images in this book and would like to investigate using them for publishing, promotions or advertising,
please visit our website www.practicalpictures.com for more information.

Publisher: Joanna Lorenz
Project Editor: Carole Clements
Copy Editor: Norma MacMillan
Designer: Sheila Volpe
Photographer: Amanda Heywood
Food Styling: Elizabeth Wolf Cohen,
steps by Marilyn Forbes and Cara Hobday

ETHICAL TRADING POLICY
At Anness Publishing we believe that business should be conducted in an ethical and ecologically sustainable way, with
respect for the environment and a proper regard to the replacement of the natural resources we employ.
As a publisher, we use a lot of wood pulp to make high-quality paper for printing, and that wood commonly comes from spruce
trees. We are therefore currently growing more than 750,000 trees in three Scottish forest plantations: Berrymoss
(130 hectares/320 acres), West Touxhill (125 hectares/305 acres) and Deveron Forest (75 hectares/185 acres). The forests we
manage contain more than 3.5 times the number of trees employed each year in making paper for the books we manufacture.
Because of this ongoing ecological investment programme, you, as our customer, can have the pleasure and reassurance of
knowing that a tree is being cultivated on your behalf to naturally replace the materials used to make the book you are holding.
Our forestry programme is run in accordance with the UK Woodland Assurance Scheme (UKWAS) and will be certified by the
internationally recognized Forest Stewardship Council (FSC). The FSC is a non-government organization dedicated to promoting
responsible management of the world's forests. Certification ensures forests are managed in an environmentally sustainable and
socially responsible way. For further information about this scheme, go to www.annesspublishing.com/trees

A CIP catalogue record for this book is available from the British Library.

Previously published as *Best of America*

PUBLISHER'S NOTE
Although the advice and information in this book are believed to be accurate and true at the time of going
to press, neither the authors nor the publisher can accept any legal responsibility or liability for any errors or
omissions that may be made nor for any inaccuracies nor for any harm or injury that comes about from
following instructions or advice in this book.

NOTES
Bracketed terms are intended for American readers.
For all recipes, quantities are given in both metric and imperial measures and, where appropriate, in standard
cups and spoons. Follow one set of measures, but not a mixture, because they are not interchangeable.
Standard spoon and cup measures are level. 1 tsp = 5ml, 1 tbsp = 15ml, 1 cup = 250ml/8fl oz.
Australian standard tablespoons are 20ml. Australian readers should use 3 tsp
in place of 1 tbsp for measuring small quantities.
American pints are 16fl oz/2 cups. American readers should use
20fl oz/2.5 cups in place of 1 pint when measuring liquids.
Electric oven temperatures in this book are for conventional ovens. When using a fan oven, the
temperature will probably need to be reduced by about 10–20°C/20–40°F. Since ovens vary, you should
check with your manufacturer's instruction book for guidance.
Medium (US large) eggs are used unless otherwise stated.

CONTENTS

INTRODUCTION 6

NEW ENGLAND & THE MID-ATLANTIC STATES 8

THE SOUTH 48

THE MIDWEST 88

THE SOUTHWEST 128

CALIFORNIA 170

THE NORTHWEST 212

INDEX 252

INTRODUCTION

American families – with their diverse culinary traditions – have always been on the move. Hardy immigrants crossed oceans, and pioneers followed a trail or a river to the West. Today they chase down jobs far from where they grew up and retire to where the sun shines. As people criss-cross the country, they adapt their favourite recipes to the local produce and, in mixed communities, adopt entirely new foods and flavours. What has evolved is the richest and most varied cuisine imaginable. Even now, new dishes are continually entering the changing repertoire.

This unique volume explores this gastronomic heritage. We take you through America's regional cooking, passing on historical tastes with vintage recipes as well as offering new dishes made with local ingredients. All the recipes are presented in a simple step-by-step format with pictures to guide you every inch of the way.

We have taken the compass points as general divisions and look at each region in terms of its most important and characteristic ingredients and its unique traditions, offering a varied and representative selection of the food from each area.

Cooking from New England and the Mid-Atlantic seaboard evokes some of America's oldest food traditions, from the first Thanksgiving to Thomas Jefferson's waffle iron. With such a long coastline, seafood has always played a key role, and cold winters promoted the hearty fare we associate with this region. For many people, the South conjures up Spanish moss, French quarter architecture, and plantations. In fact, the Spanish, French, and African-American influences are the most important ones in terms of local food, and Cajun, Creole, and soul food mingle with customs of gracious dining carried over from earlier times.

Moving westward, the Midwest has always been the breadbasket of the country and, although much fertile farmland has been urbanized today, raising crops and animals for the table is still important. The Southwest draws on heirloom traditions, gleaned from Native Americans and Spanish settlers of the areas. Since the state of California occupies much of the West coast and has had such an influence on culinary trends, we have treated it on its own. With well stocked coastal waters and orchards laden with apples, the Pacific Northwest and the Mountain States conclude the culinary tour.

Today cooking at home has changed from an everyday event starting from scratch to more of a hobby. But whether you're preparing for a festive meal to share with friends or simply putting together a quick dinner, this wonderful cookbook has recipes to suit.

NEW ENGLAND & THE MID-ATLANTIC STATES

THE FIRST SETTLERS FOUND REFUGE IN THIS PART OF THE COUNTRY AND WORKED THE FERTILE LAND, CREATING A RICH CULINARY HERITAGE. SINCE COLONIAL DAYS, THE TRADITION OF GOOD EATING THAT DEVELOPED HERE SPREAD TO OTHER AREAS. WITH SO MUCH COASTLINE, SEAFOOD HAS ALWAYS BEEN A KEY INGREDIENT IN THE COOKING OF THIS REGION.

New England Clam Chowder

SERVES 8

48 clams, such as cherrystone or littleneck, scrubbed

1.3 litres/2¼ pints/6 cups water

40g/1½oz/¼ cup finely diced salt pork

3 onions, finely chopped

1 bay leaf

5 potatoes, diced

salt and pepper

475ml/16fl oz/2 cups milk, warmed

250ml/8fl oz/1 cup single (light) cream

chopped fresh parsley, to garnish

1 Rinse the clams well in cold water. Drain. Place them in a deep pan with the water and bring to the boil. Cover and steam until the shells open, about 10 minutes. Remove the pan from the heat.

2 When the clams have cooled slightly, remove them from their shells. Discard any clams that have not opened. Chop the clams coarsely. Strain the cooking liquid through a strainer lined with muslin (cheesecloth), and reserve it.

3 In a large heavy pan, fry the salt pork until it renders its fat and begins to brown. Add the onions and cook over a low heat until softened, 8–10 minutes.

4 ▲ Add the bay leaf, potatoes and clam cooking liquid. Stir. Bring to the boil and cook for 5–10 minutes.

5 ▲ Stir in the chopped clams. Continue to cook until the potatoes are tender, stirring occasionally. Season with salt and pepper.

6 Reduce the heat to low and stir in the warmed milk and cream. Simmer very gently for 5 minutes more. Discard the bay leaf, and taste and adjust the seasoning before serving, sprinkled with parsley.

~ COOK'S TIP ~

If clams have been dug, purging helps to rid them of sand and stomach contents. Put them in a bowl of cold water, sprinkle with 50g/2oz/½ cup cornmeal and some salt. Stir lightly and leave to stand in a cool place for 3–4 hours.

Chilled Asparagus Soup

SERVES 6

900g/2lb fresh asparagus

60ml/4 tbsp butter or olive oil

175g/6oz/1½ cups sliced leeks or spring
onions (scallions)

45ml/3 tbsp plain (all-purpose) flour

1.5 litres/2½ pints/6¼ cups chicken stock

salt and pepper

½ cup single (light) cream

15ml/1 tbsp finely chopped fresh
tarragon or chervil

1 ▲ Cut the top 6cm/2½in off the
asparagus spears. Blanch these tips in
boiling water until just tender, about
5–6 minutes. Drain. Cut each tip into
two or three pieces, and set aside.

2 Trim the ends of the stalks,
removing any brown or woody parts.
Chop the stalks into 1cm/½in pieces.

3 ▲ Heat the butter or oil in a heavy
pan. Add the leeks or spring onions
and cook over a low heat until softened,
5–8 minutes. Stir in the chopped
asparagus stalks, cover and cook for
6–8 minutes more.

4 Add the flour and stir well to blend.
Cook for 3–4 minutes, uncovered, stirring occasionally.

5 ▼ Add the chicken stock. Bring to
the boil, stirring frequently, then
reduce the heat and simmer for 30
minutes. Season with salt and pepper.

6 ▲ Purée the soup in a food processor
or blender. If necessary, strain it to
remove any coarse fibres. Stir in the
asparagus tips, most of the cream and
the herbs. Chill well. Stir thoroughly
before serving, and check the seasoning. Garnish with swirled cream to
make an attractive pattern, then serve.

Chesapeake Melon and Crab Meat Salad

Serves 6

450g/1lb fresh crab meat

115g/4oz/½ cup mayonnaise

50ml/2fl oz/¼ cup sour cream or natural (plain) yogurt

30ml/2 tbsp olive oil

30ml/2 tbsp fresh lemon or lime juice

20g/¾oz/¼ cup finely chopped spring onions (scallions)

30ml/2 tbsp finely chopped fresh coriander (cilantro)

1.5ml/¼ tsp cayenne pepper

salt and pepper

1½ canteloupe or small honeydew melons

3 heads of Belgian endive

fresh coriander sprigs, to garnish

1 ▲ Pick over the crab meat very carefully, removing any bits of shell or cartilage. Leave the pieces of crab meat as large as possible.

2 ▲ In a medium bowl, combine all the other ingredients except the melon and endive. Mix well. Fold the crab meat into this dressing.

3 ▲ Halve the melons and remove the seeds. Cut into thin slices and remove the rind.

4 ▲ Arrange the salad on individual serving plates, making a decorative design with the melon slices and whole endive leaves. Place a mound of dressed crab meat on each plate. Garnish each salad with fresh coriander sprigs.

Long Island Scallop and Mussel Kebabs

SERVES 4

65g/2½oz/5 tbsp butter,
  at room temperature

30ml/2 tbsp finely chopped fresh fennel
  fronds or parsley

15ml/1 tbsp fresh lemon juice

salt and pepper

32 bay or small scallops

24 large mussels in shell

8 bacon rashers (strips)

50g/2oz/1 cup fresh breadcrumbs

50ml/2fl oz/¼ cup olive oil

hot toast, to serve

1 ▲ Make the flavoured butter by combining the butter with the chopped herbs, lemon juice and salt and pepper to taste. Mix well. Set aside.

2 ▲ In a small pan, cook the scallops in their own liquor until they begin to shrink. (If there is no scallop liquor – retained from the shells after shelling – use a little fish stock or white wine.) Drain and pat dry with kitchen paper.

3 Scrub the mussels well, and rinse under cold running water. Place in a large pan with about 2.5cm/1in of water in the bottom. Cover and steam the mussels over a medium heat until they open. Remove them from their shells, and pat dry on kitchen paper. Discard any mussels that have not opened.

4 ▼ Take eight 15cm/6in wooden or metal skewers. Thread on each one, alternately, four scallops, three mussels and a rasher of bacon, weaving the bacon between the scallops and mussels.

5 Preheat the grill (broiler).

6 ▲ Spread the breadcrumbs on a plate. Brush the seafood with olive oil and roll in the crumbs to coat all over.

7 Place the skewers on the grill (broiling) rack. Grill (broil) until crisp and lightly browned, 4–5 minutes on each side. Serve at once with hot toast and the flavoured butter.

Oyster Stew

SERVES 6

475ml/16fl oz/2 cups milk

475ml/16fl oz/2 cups single (light) cream

1.2 litres/2 pints shelled oysters, drained, with their liquor reserved

pinch of paprika

salt and pepper

25g/1oz/2 tbsp butter

15ml/1 tbsp finely chopped fresh parsley

1 Combine the milk, cream and oyster liquor in a heavy pan.

2 ▼ Heat the mixture over a medium heat until small bubbles appear around the edge of the pan. Do not allow it to boil. Reduce the heat to low and add the oysters.

3 Cook, stirring occasionally, until the oysters plump up and their edges begin to curl. Add the paprika, and salt and pepper to taste.

4 Meanwhile, warm six soup plates or bowls. Cut the butter into six pieces and put one piece in each bowl.

5 Ladle in the oyster stew and sprinkle with the chopped parsley. Serve at once.

Oysters Rockefeller

SERVES 6

450g/1lb fresh spinach leaves

40g/1½oz/½ cup chopped spring onions (scallions)

50g/2oz/½ cup chopped celery

25g/1oz/½ cup chopped fresh parsley

1 garlic clove

2 anchovy fillets

50g/2oz/¼ cup butter or margarine

30g/1¼oz/½ cup dried breadcrumbs

5ml/1 tsp Worcestershire sauce

30ml/2 tbsp anise-flavoured liqueur (Pernod or Ricard)

2.5ml/½ tsp salt

hot pepper sauce

36 oysters in the shell

fine strips of lemon rind, to garnish

~ COOK'S TIP ~

To open an oyster, push the point of an oyster knife about 1cm/½in into the "hinge". Push down firmly. The lid should pop open.

1 ▲ Wash the spinach well. Drain, and place in a heavy pan. Cover and cook over a low heat until just wilted. Remove from the heat. When the spinach is cool enough to handle, squeeze it to remove the excess water.

2 ▲ Put the spinach, spring onions, celery, parsley, garlic and anchovy fillets in a food processor and process until finely chopped.

3 Heat the butter or margarine in a frying pan. Add the spinach mixture, breadcrumbs, Worcestershire sauce, liqueur, salt and hot sauce to taste. Cook for 1–2 minutes. Cool, then chill.

4 Preheat the oven to 230°C/450°F/ Gas 8. Line a baking sheet with crumpled foil.

5 ▲ Open the oysters and remove the top shells. Arrange them, side by side, on the foil (it will keep them upright). Spoon the spinach mixture over the oysters, smoothing the tops with the back of the spoon.

6 Bake until piping hot, about 20 minutes. Serve at once, garnished with the lemon rind.

Oyster Stew (top), Oysters Rockefeller

Cape Cod Fried Clams

SERVES 4

36 clams, such as cherrystone, scrubbed

250ml/8fl oz/1 cup buttermilk

pinch of celery salt

1.5ml/¼ tsp cayenne pepper

oil for deep-frying

65g/2½oz/1 cup dried breadcrumbs

2 eggs, beaten with 30ml/2 tbsp water

lemon wedges and tartare sauce or
    tomato ketchup, to serve

1 Rinse the clams well. Put them in a large pan with 475ml/16fl oz/2 cups water and bring to the boil. Cover and steam until the shells open.

2 ▼ Remove the clams from their shells, and cut away the black skins from the necks. Discard any clams that have not opened. Strain the cooking liquid and reserve.

3 ▲ Place the buttermilk in a large bowl and stir in the celery salt and cayenne. Add the clams and 120ml/4fl oz/½ cup of their cooking liquid. Mix well. Leave to stand for 1 hour.

4 Heat the oil in a deep-fryer or large pan to 190°C/375°F. (To test the temperature without a thermometer, drop in a cube of bread; it should be golden brown in 40 seconds.)

5 ▲ Drain the clams and roll them in the breadcrumbs to coat all over. Dip them in the beaten egg and then in the breadcrumbs again.

6 Fry the clams in the hot oil, a few at a time, stirring, until they are crisp and brown, about 2 minutes per batch. Remove with a slotted spoon and drain on kitchen paper.

7 Serve the fried clams hot, accompanied by lemon wedges and tartare sauce or ketchup.

Eggs Benedict

SERVES 4

5ml/1 tsp vinegar

4 eggs

2 English muffins or 4 slices of bread

butter, for spreading

2 slices of cooked ham, 5mm/¼in thick,
  each cut in half crossways

fresh chives, to garnish

FOR THE SAUCE

3 egg yolks

30ml/2 tbsp fresh lemon juice

1.5ml/¼ tsp salt

115g/4oz/½ cup butter

30ml/2 tbsp single (light) cream

pepper

4 ▼ Bring a shallow pan of water to the boil. Stir in the vinegar. Break each egg into a cup, then slide it carefully into the water. Delicately turn the white around the yolk with a slotted spoon. Cook until the egg is set to your taste, 3–4 minutes. Remove to kitchen paper to drain. Very gently cut any ragged edges off the eggs with a small knife or scissors.

5 ▲ While the eggs are poaching, split and toast the muffins or toast the bread slices. Butter while still warm.

6 Place a piece of ham, which you may brown in butter if you wish, on each muffin half or slice of toast. Trim the ham to fit neatly. Place an egg on each ham-topped muffin. Spoon the warm sauce over the eggs, garnish with chives and serve.

1 ▲ For the sauce, put the egg yolks, lemon juice and salt in the container of a food processor or blender. Blend for 15 seconds.

2 Melt the butter in a small pan until it bubbles (do not let it brown). With the motor running, pour the hot butter into the food processor or blender through the feed tube in a slow, steady stream. Turn off the machine as soon as all the butter has been added.

3 Scrape the sauce into the top of a double boiler over just simmering water, or a heatproof bowl set over hot water. Stir until thickened, about 2–3 minutes. (If the sauce curdles, whisk in 15ml/1 tbsp boiling water.) Stir in the cream and season with pepper. Keep warm over the hot water.

Maryland Crab Cakes with Tartare Sauce

SERVES 4

675g/1½lb fresh crab meat

1 egg, beaten

30ml/2 tbsp mayonnaise

15ml/1 tbsp Worcestershire sauce

15ml/1 tbsp sherry

30ml/2 tbsp finely chopped fresh parsley

15ml/1 tbsp finely chopped fresh chives

salt and pepper

45ml/3 tbsp olive oil

FOR THE SAUCE

1 egg yolk

15ml/1 tbsp white wine vinegar

30ml/2 tbsp Dijon-style mustard

250ml/8fl oz/1 cup vegetable oil

30ml/2 tbsp fresh lemon juice

20g/¾oz/¼ cup finely chopped spring
   onions (scallions)

30ml/2 tbsp chopped drained capers

few finely chopped sour dill pickles

60ml/4 tbsp finely chopped fresh parsley

1 ▲ Pick over the crab meat, removing any shell or cartilage. Keep the pieces of crab as large as possible.

~ COOK'S TIP ~

For easier handling and to make the crab meat go further, add 50g/2oz/ 1 cup fresh breadcrumbs and one more egg to the crab mixture. Divide the mixture into 12 cakes to serve six.

2 ▲ In a mixing bowl, combine the beaten egg with the mayonnaise, Worcestershire sauce, sherry and herbs. Season with salt and pepper. Gently fold in the crab meat.

3 ▲ Divide the mixture into eight portions and gently form each one into an oval cake. Place on a baking sheet between layers of baking parchment and chill for at least 1 hour.

4 ▲ Meanwhile, make the sauce. In a medium bowl, beat the egg yolk with a wire whisk until smooth. Add the vinegar, mustard and salt and pepper to taste, and whisk for about 10 seconds to blend. Whisk in the oil in a slow, steady stream.

5 ▲ Add the lemon juice, spring onions, capers, pickles and parsley and mix well. Check the seasoning. Cover and chill.

6 Preheat the grill (broiler).

7 ▲ Brush the crab cakes with the olive oil. Place on an oiled baking sheet, in one layer.

8 ▲ Grill (broil) 15cm/6in from the heat until golden brown, about 5 minutes on each side. Serve the crab cakes hot with the tartare sauce.

Baked Fish

SERVES 6

1.2kg/2½lb cod, haddock or bluefish fillets, skinned

45ml/3 tbsp olive oil

5ml/1 tsp drained capers

2 garlic cloves

2 ripe tomatoes, peeled, seeded and finely diced

30ml/2 tbsp finely chopped fresh basil, or 10ml/1 tsp dried basil

salt and pepper

250ml/8fl oz/1 cup dry white wine

1 Preheat the oven to 200°C/400°F/ Gas 6.

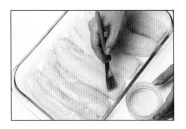

2 ▲ Arrange the fillets in one layer in a shallow oiled baking dish. Brush the fish with olive oil.

3 Chop the capers with the garlic. Mix with the tomatoes and basil. Season with salt and pepper.

4 ▼ Spoon the tomato mixture over the fish. Pour in the wine. Bake until the fish is cooked, 15–20 minutes. Test to see if the fish is done with the point of a knife; the fish should be just opaque in the centre. Serve hot.

Old Westbury Flounder with Crab

SERVES 6

50g/2oz/¼ cup butter or margarine

25g/1oz/¼ cup plain (all-purpose) flour

250ml/8fl oz/1 cup fish stock, or 175ml/ 6fl oz/¾ cup fish stock mixed with 50ml/2fl oz/¼ cup dry white wine

250ml/8fl oz/1 cup milk

1 bay leaf

salt and pepper

12 flounder fillets, about 1.2kg/2½lb

250g/9oz/1½ cups fresh crab meat, flaked

40g/1½oz/½ cup freshly grated Parmesan

1 Preheat the oven to 220°C/425°F/ Gas 7.

~ VARIATIONS ~

Other flat white fish, such as sole, can be substituted for the flounder. Raw peeled and deveined prawns (shrimp), chopped if large, can be used instead of crab meat.

2 ▲ In a medium heavy pan, melt the butter or margarine over a medium heat. Stir in the flour and cook for 2–3 minutes.

3 ▲ Pour in the fish stock (or mixed fish stock and wine) and the milk. Whisk until smooth.

4 Add the bay leaf. Raise the heat to medium-high and bring to the boil. Cook for 3–4 minutes more. Remove the sauce from the heat, and add salt to taste. Keep hot.

5 ▲ Butter a large baking dish. Twist each fillet to form a "cone" shape and arrange in the dish. Sprinkle the crab meat over the fish. Pour the hot sauce evenly over the top and sprinkle with the cheese.

6 Bake until the top is golden brown and the fish is cooked, 10–12 minutes. Test to see if the fish is done with the point of a knife: the fish should be just opaque in the centre. Serve hot.

Baked Fish (top), Old Westbury Flounder with Crab

Scallops Thermidor

SERVES 6

900g/2lb scallops
50g/2oz/½ cup plain (all-purpose) flour
115g/4oz/½ cup butter or margarine
65g/2½oz/1 cup quartered small mushrooms
25g/1oz/½ cup fresh breadcrumbs
30ml/2 tbsp finely chopped fresh parsley
30ml/2 tbsp finely chopped fresh chives
120ml/4fl oz/½ cup sherry
50ml/2fl oz/¼ cup cognac
5ml/1 tsp Worcestershire sauce
2.5ml/½ tsp salt
1.5ml/¼ tsp black pepper
350ml/12fl oz/1½ cups whipping cream
2 egg yolks
chives, to garnish (optional)

1 Preheat oven to 200°C/400°F/Gas 6.

2 ▲ Roll the scallops in the flour, shaking off the excess. Heat half the butter or margarine in a medium frying pan. Add the scallops and sauté until they are barely golden all over, about 3 minutes. Remove from the pan and set aside.

3 ▲ Melt two more tablespoons of butter or margarine in the pan. Add the mushrooms and breadcrumbs and sauté for 3–4 minutes, stirring. Add the parsley, chives, sherry, cognac, Worcestershire sauce and salt and pepper. Cook for 3–4 minutes more, stirring well.

4 ▲ Add the cream, and cook for another 3–4 minutes, stirring occasionally. Remove from the heat and mix in the egg yolks. Fold in the sautéed scallops.

5 Divide the mixture among six greased individual gratin or other baking dishes. Or, if you prefer, put it all in one large shallow baking dish. Dot with the remaining 30ml/2 tbsp butter or margarine.

6 Bake until bubbling and lightly browned, about 10 minutes. Serve at once in the dishes. Garnish with chives, if you wish.

Spaghetti with Clams

SERVES 4

24 hard-shell clams, such as littlenecks, scrubbed

250ml/8fl oz/1 cup water

120ml/4fl oz/½ cup dry white wine

salt and pepper

450g/1lb spaghetti, preferably Italian

75ml/5 tbsp olive oil

2 garlic cloves, finely chopped

45ml/3 tbsp finely chopped fresh parsley

1 ▲ Rinse the clams well in cold water and drain. Place in a large pan with the water and wine and bring to the boil. Cover and steam until the shells open, about 6–8 minutes.

2 Discard any clams that have not opened. Remove the clams from their shells. If large, chop them roughly.

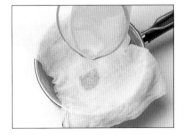

3 ▲ Strain the cooking liquid through a strainer lined with muslin (cheesecloth). Place in a small pan and boil rapidly until it has reduced by about half. Set aside.

4 Bring a large pan of water to the boil. Add 5ml/1 tsp salt. When the water is boiling rapidly, add the spaghetti and stir well as it softens. Cook until the spaghetti is almost done, and still firm to the bite (check the packet instructions for cooking times).

5 ▼ Meanwhile, heat the olive oil in a large frying pan. Add the garlic and cook for 2–3 minutes, but do not let it brown. Add the reduced clam liquid and the parsley. Let it cook over a low heat until the spaghetti is ready.

6 ▲ Drain the spaghetti. Add it to the frying pan, raise the heat to medium and add the clams. Cook for 3–4 minutes, stirring constantly to cover the spaghetti with the sauce and to heat the clams.

7 Season with salt and pepper and serve. No cheese is needed with this clam sauce.

Maine Grilled Lobster Dinner

SERVES 4

4 live lobsters, about 675g/1½lb each

45ml/3 tbsp finely chopped mixed fresh
 herbs, such as parsley, chives
 and tarragon

225g/8oz/1 cup butter, melted and
 kept warm

8 tender corn on the cob, cleaned

salt and pepper

lemon halves, to garnish

1 Preheat the grill (broiler).

2 Kill each lobster quickly by
inserting the tip of a large chef's knife
between the eyes.

3 ▲ Turn the lobster over on to its
back and cut it in half, from the head
straight down to the tail. Remove and
discard the hard sac near the head,
and the intestinal vein that runs
through the middle of the underside of
the tail. All the rest of the lobster meat
is edible. Preheat the grill (broiler).

4 ▲ Combine the finely chopped
herbs with the melted butter.

5 ▲ Place the lobster halves, shell side
up, in a foil-lined grill (broiling) pan or
a large roasting pan. (You may have to
do this in two batches.) Grill (broil) for
about 8 minutes. Turn the lobster halves
over, brush generously with the herb
butter, and grill for 7–8 minutes more.

6 ▲ While the lobsters are cooking,
drop the corn cobs into a large pan of
rapidly boiling water and cook until
just tender, 4–7 minutes. Drain.

7 Serve the lobsters and corn hot,
with salt, freshly ground black pepper,
lemon halves and individual bowls of
herb butter. Provide crackers for the
claws, extra plates for cobs and shells,
finger bowls and lots of napkins.

Prawn Soufflé

SERVES 4–6

15ml/1 tbsp dried breadcrumbs

25g/1oz/2 tbsp butter or margarine

90g/3½oz/⅔ cup coarsely chopped cooked prawns (shrimp)

15ml/1 tbsp finely chopped fresh tarragon or parsley

1.5ml/¼ tsp pepper

45ml/3 tbsp sherry or dry white wine

FOR THE SOUFFLÉ MIXTURE

40g/1½oz/3 tbsp butter or margarine

37 ml/2½ tbsp plain (all-purpose) flour

250ml/8fl oz/1 cup milk, heated

4ml/¾ tsp salt

4 eggs, separated, plus 1 white

1 ▲ Butter a 1.5–2 litre/2½–3½ pint soufflé dish. Sprinkle with the bread-crumbs, tilting the dish to coat the bottom and sides evenly.

2 Preheat the oven to 200°C/400°F/ Gas 6.

~ VARIATIONS ~

For Lobster Soufflé, substitute 1 large lobster tail for the cooked prawns (shrimp). Chop it finely and add to the pan with the herbs and wine in place of the prawns. For Crab Soufflé, use 175g/6oz/1 cup fresh crab meat, picked over carefully to remove any bits of shell and cartilage, in place of the prawns.

3 ▲ Melt the butter or margarine in a small pan. Add the chopped prawns and cook for 2–3 minutes over a low heat. Stir in the herbs, pepper and wine and cook for 1–2 minutes more. Raise the heat and boil rapidly to evaporate the liquid. Remove from the heat and set aside.

4 For the soufflé mixture, melt the butter or margarine in a medium heavy pan. Add the flour, blending it well with a wire whisk. Cook over a low heat for 2–3 minutes. Pour in the hot milk and whisk vigorously until smooth. Simmer for 2 minutes, still whisking. Stir in the salt.

5 ▼ Remove from the heat and immediately beat in the egg yolks, one at a time. Stir in the prawn mixture.

6 In a large bowl, whisk the egg whites until they form stiff peaks. Stir about one-quarter of the egg whites into the prawn mixture. Gently fold in the rest of the egg whites.

7 Turn the mixture into the prepared dish. Place in the oven and reduce the heat to 190°C/375°F/Gas 5. Bake until the soufflé is puffed up and lightly browned on top, 30–40 minutes. Serve at once.

Chicken Brunswick Stew

SERVES 6

1.8kg/4lb chicken, cut into
   serving pieces

paprika, for dusting

30ml/2 tbsp olive oil

25g/1oz/2 tbsp butter

4 onions, chopped

225g/8oz/1 cup chopped green or yellow
   (bell) pepper

450g/1lb/2 cups chopped peeled fresh or
   canned plum tomatoes

250ml/8fl oz/1 cup white wine

475ml/16fl oz/2 cups chicken stock
   or water

15g/½oz/¼ cup chopped fresh parsley

2.5ml/½ tsp hot pepper sauce

15ml/1 tbsp Worcestershire sauce

2 cups corn kernels, fresh, frozen
   or canned

150g/5oz/1 cup butter (lima) beans

45ml/3 tbsp plain (all-purpose) flour

salt and pepper

savoury scones, rice or potatoes, to serve
   (optional)

1 ▲ Rinse the chicken pieces under cool water and pat dry with kitchen paper. Dust each piece lightly with salt and paprika.

2 In a large heavy pan, heat the olive oil with the butter over a medium-high heat. Heat until the mixture is sizzling and just starting to change colour.

3 ▲ Add the chicken pieces and fry until golden brown on all sides. Remove the chicken pieces with tongs and set aside.

4 ▲ Reduce the heat to low and add the onions and pepper to the pan. Cook until softened, 8–10 minutes.

5 Raise the heat. Add the tomatoes and their juice, the wine, stock or water, parsley and hot pepper and Worcestershire sauces. Stir and bring to the boil.

6 ▲ Return the chicken to the pan, pushing it down into the sauce. Cover, reduce the heat and simmer for 30 minutes, stirring occasionally.

7 ▲ Add the corn and butter beans and mix well. Partly cover and cook for 30 minutes more.

8 ▲ Tilt the pan, and skim off as much of the surface fat as possible. In a small bowl, mix the flour with a little water to make a paste.

9 ▲ Gradually stir in about 175ml/ 6fl oz/¾ cup of the hot sauce from the pan. Stir the flour mixture into the stew, and mix well to distribute it evenly. Cook for 5–8 minutes more, stirring occasionally.

10 Check the seasoning. Serve the stew in shallow soup plates, with scones, rice or potatoes, if you like.

Yankee Pot Roast

SERVES 8

1.8kg/4lb chuck steak, rump (round) steak or brisket

3 garlic cloves, cut in half or in thirds

225g/8oz piece of salt pork

4 onions, chopped

115g/4oz/1 cup chopped celery

4–6 carrots, chopped

150g/5oz/1 cup diced turnips

475ml/16fl oz/2 cups beef or chicken stock

475ml/16fl oz/2 cups dry red or white wine

1 bay leaf

5ml/1 tsp fresh thyme leaves, or 2.5ml/½ tsp dried thyme

8 small potatoes

2.5ml/½ tsp salt

2.5ml/½ tsp pepper

50g/2oz/¼ cup butter or margarine, at room temperature

25g/1oz/¼ cup plain (all-purpose) flour

watercress, to garnish

1 Preheat the oven to 160°F/325°F/Gas 3.

2 ▲ With the tip of a sharp knife, make deep incisions in the meat, on all sides, and insert the garlic pieces.

3 In a large, lidded flameproof casserole, cook the salt pork over a low heat until it renders its fat and begins to brown.

4 ▲ Remove the salt pork with a slotted spoon and discard. Raise the heat to medium-high and add the steak or brisket. Brown it on all sides. Remove and set aside.

5 ▲ Add the onions, celery and carrots to the casserole and cook over a low heat until softened, 8–10 minutes. Stir in the turnips. Add the stock, wine and herbs and mix well. Return the steak. Cover and place in the oven. Cook for 2 hours.

6 ▲ Add the potatoes, pushing them down under the other vegetables. Season with salt and pepper. Cover again and cook until the potatoes are tender, about 45 minutes.

7 ▲ In a small bowl, combine the butter or margarine with the flour and mash together to make a paste.

8 Transfer the meat to a warmed serving dish. Remove the potatoes and other vegetables from the casserole with a slotted spoon and arrange around the roast. Keep hot.

9 ▲ Discard the bay leaf. Tilt the casserole and skim off the excess fat from the surface of the cooking liquid. Bring to the boil on top of the stove. Add half the butter and flour paste and whisk to blend. Cook until the gravy is thickened, 3–4 minutes. Add more of the paste if the gravy is not sufficiently thick. Strain into a gravy boat. Serve with the sliced meat and vegetables, garnished with watercress.

~ VARIATION ~

Add 175g/6oz/1½ cups frozen peas to the casserole about 5 minutes before the potatoes are done.

Philadelphia Scrapple

SERVES 10

1.3kg/3lb pork neck bones or
    pigs' knuckles

3.5 litres/6 pints water

5ml/1 tsp salt

1 bay leaf

2 fresh sage leaves

5ml/1 tsp pepper

300g/11oz/2¾ cups yellow cornmeal

maple syrup, fried eggs and grilled
    (broiled) tomatoes, to serve (optional)

1 Put the bones or knuckles, water,
salt and herbs in a large pan. Bring to
the boil and simmer for 2 hours.

2 ▲ Remove the meat from the
bones and chop it finely or mince it.
Set aside. Strain the broth and skim
off any fat from the surface. Discard
the bones.

3 Put 2.4 litres/4 pints of the broth in
a large heavy pan. Add the chopped or
minced meat and the pepper. Bring to
the boil.

4 ▲ There should be about 1.2 litres/
2 pints of broth left. Stir the cornmeal
into this. Add to the boiling mixture
in the pan and cook until thickened,
about 10 minutes, stirring constantly.

5 Reduce the heat to very low, cover
the pan and continue cooking for
about 25 minutes, stirring often. Check
the seasoning.

6 ▲ Turn the mixture into two loaf
tins and smooth the surface. Leave to
cool, then chill overnight.

7 To serve, cut the loaves into 1cm/
½in slices. Sprinkle with flour and
brown on both sides in butter or other
fat over a medium heat. Serve with
warmed maple syrup, fried eggs and
grilled tomato halves, if you wish.

Red Flannel Hash with Corned Beef

SERVES 4

6 bacon rashers (strips)

175g/6oz/¾ cup finely chopped onion

5 potatoes, boiled and diced

250g/9oz/1½ cups chopped corned beef

350g/12oz/1½ cups diced cooked
  beetroot (beet) (not in vinegar)

50ml/2fl oz/¼ cup single (light) or
  pouring (half-and-half) cream

15g/½oz/¼ cup finely chopped
  fresh parsley, plus sprig to garnish

salt and pepper

1 ▲ Cook the bacon in a large heavy
or nonstick frying pan until golden and
beginning to crisp. Remove with a
slotted spatula and drain on kitchen
paper. Pour off all but 30ml/2 tbsp
of the bacon fat in the pan, reserving
the rest for later.

2 ▲ Cut the bacon into 1cm/½in
pieces and place in a mixing bowl.
Cook the onion in the bacon fat over a
low heat until softened, 8–10 minutes.
Remove it from the pan and add to the
bacon. Mix in the potatoes, corned
beef, beetroot, cream and the finely
chopped parsley. Season with salt and
pepper and mix well.

3 ▼ Heat 60ml/4 tbsp of the reserved
bacon fat, or other fat, in the frying
pan. Add the hash mixture, spreading
it out evenly with a spatula. Cook over
a low heat until the bottom is brown,
about 15 minutes. Flip the hash out on
to a plate.

4 ▲ Gently slide the hash back into
the frying pan and cook on the other
side until lightly browned. Serve at
once, garnished with the parsley sprig.

Boston Baked Beans

SERVES 8

3 cups dried haricot (navy) or
  Great Northern beans

1 bay leaf

4 cloves

2 onions, peeled

185g/6½oz/½ cup treacle (molasses)

150g/5oz/¾ cup soft dark brown sugar

15ml/1 tbsp Dijon-style mustard

5ml/1 tsp salt

5ml/1 tsp pepper

250ml/8fl oz/1 cup boiling water

225g/8oz piece of salt pork

1 Rinse the beans under cold running water. Drain and place in a large bowl. Cover with cold water and leave to soak overnight. Drain and rinse again.

2 Put the beans in a large pan with the bay leaf and cover with fresh cold water. Bring to the boil and simmer until tender, 1½–2 hours. Drain.

3 Preheat the oven to 140°C/275°F/ Gas 1.

4 ▲ Put the beans in a large casserole. Stick two cloves in each of the onions and add them to the pan.

5 In a mixing bowl, combine the treacle, dark brown sugar, mustard, salt and pepper. Add the boiling water and stir to blend.

6 Pour this mixture over the beans. Add more water if necessary so the beans are almost covered with liquid.

7 ▲ Blanch the piece of salt pork in boiling water for 3 minutes. Drain. Score the rind in deep 1cm/½in cuts. Add the salt pork to the casserole and push down just below the surface of the beans, skin-side up.

8 Cover the casserole and bake in the centre of the oven for 4½–5 hours. Uncover for the last half hour, so the pork rind becomes brown and crisp. Slice or shred the pork and serve hot.

Harvard Beetroot

SERVES 6

5 cooked beetroot (beets),
  about 675g/1½lb

75g/3oz/6 tbsp granulated sugar

15ml/1 tbsp cornflour (cornstarch)

2.5ml/½ tsp salt

50ml/2fl oz/¼ cup cider or
  white wine vinegar

120ml/4fl oz/½ cup beetroot cooking
  liquid or water

25g/1oz/2 tbsp butter or margarine

1 Peel the beetroot and cut into medium-thick slices. Set aside.

2 ▲ In the top of a double boiler, combine all the other ingredients except the butter or margarine. Stir until smooth. Cook over hot water, stirring constantly, until the mixture is smooth and clear.

3 ▼ Add the beetroot and butter or margarine. Continue to cook over the hot water, stirring occasionally, until the beetroot slices are heated through, about 10 minutes. Serve hot.

Boston Baked Beans (top), Harvard Beetroot

Coleslaw

Serves 8

225g/8oz/1 cup mayonnaise

120ml/4fl oz/½ cup white wine vinegar

15ml/1 tbsp Dijon-style mustard

10ml/2 tsp caster (superfine) sugar

15ml/1 tbsp caraway seeds

salt and pepper

900g/2lb/8 cups grated green cabbage,
    or a mixture of green and red cabbage

150g/5oz/1 cup grated carrots

2 yellow or red onions, finely sliced

1 Combine the mayonnaise, vinegar, mustard, sugar and caraway seeds. Season with salt and pepper.

2 ▼ Put the cabbage, carrots and onions in a large bowl.

3 ▲ Add the dressing to the vegetables and mix well. Taste for seasoning. Cover and chill for 1–2 hours. The cabbage will become more tender the longer it marinates.

Pennsylvania Dutch Fried Tomatoes

Serves 4

2–3 large green or very firm red tomatoes

40g/1½oz/⅓ cup plain (all-purpose) flour

50g/2oz/¼ cup butter or bacon fat

granulated sugar, if needed

4 slices hot buttered toast

175ml/6fl oz/¾ cup pouring
    (half-and-half) cream

salt and pepper

1 ▼ Slice the tomatoes into 1cm/½in rounds. Coat lightly with flour.

2 ▲ Heat the butter or bacon fat in a frying pan. When it is hot, add the tomato slices and cook until browned. Turn them once, and season generously with salt and pepper.

3 If the tomatoes are green, sprinkle each slice with a little sugar. Cook until the other side is brown, about 3–4 minutes more.

4 Divide the tomatoes among the slices of toast and keep hot.

5 ▲ Pour the cream into the hot frying pan and bring to the boil. Simmer for 1–2 minutes, stirring to mix in the brown bits and cooking juices. Spoon the gravy over the tomatoes, and serve at once.

> ### ~ VARIATION ~
>
> For Fried Tomatoes with Ham, top the toast with ham slices before covering with the tomatoes.

Coleslaw (top), Pennsylvania Dutch Fried Tomatoes

Boston Brown Bread

MAKES 2 SMALL LOAVES

15ml/1 tbsp butter or margarine, softened

115g/4oz/1 cup yellow cornmeal

115g/4oz/1 cup wholemeal
(whole-wheat) flour

115g/4oz/1 cup rye flour

5ml/1 tsp bicarbonate of soda
(baking soda)

5ml/1 tsp salt

475ml/16fl oz/2 cups buttermilk

275g/10oz/¾ cup treacle

175g/6oz/1 cup chopped raisins

butter or cream cheese, to serve

1 ▲ Grease two 450g/1lb food cans,
or two 1.2 litre/2 pint pudding dishes,
with the soft butter or margarine.

2 ▲ Sift all the dry ingredients
together into a large bowl. Tip in any
bran from the wholemeal flour. Stir
well to blend.

3 In a separate bowl, combine the
buttermilk, treacle and raisins. Add to
the dry ingredients and mix well.

4 ▲ Pour the mixture into the
prepared cans, filling them about
two-thirds full. Cover the tops with
buttered foil, and tie or tape it down
so that the rising bread cannot push
the foil lid off.

5 Set the cans on a rack in a large pan
with a tight-fitting lid. Pour in enough
warm water to come halfway up the
sides of the cans. Cover the pan, bring
to the boil and steam for 2½ hours.
Check occasionally that the water has
not boiled away, and add more if
necessary to keep the level up.

6 Turn the bread out on to a warmed
serving dish. Slice and serve with
butter or cream cheese for spreading.

Sweet Potato Scones

Makes about 24

150g/5oz/1¼ cups plain (all-purpose) flour

20ml/4 tsp baking powder

5ml/1 tsp salt

15ml/1 tbsp brown sugar

65g/2½oz/¼ cup mashed cooked
    sweet potatoes

150ml/¼ pint/⅔ cup milk

60ml/4 tbsp melted butter or margarine

1 Preheat the oven to 230°C/450°F/
Gas 8.

2 ▲ Sift the flour, baking powder
and salt into a bowl. Add the sugar
and stir to mix.

3 ▲ In a separate bowl, combine the
sweet potato mash with the milk and
melted butter or margarine. Mix well
until evenly blended.

4 ▼ Stir the dry ingredients into the
sweet potato mixture to make a
dough. Turn out on to a lightly floured
surface and knead lightly just to mix,
1–2 minutes.

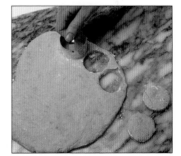

5 ▲ Roll or pat out the scone mixure
to 1cm/½in thickness. Cut out rounds
with a 4cm/1½in pastry (cookie) cutter.

6 Arrange the rounds on a greased
baking sheet. Bake until puffed and
lightly golden, about 15 minutes.
Serve the scones warm.

Boston Cream Pie

Serves 8

225g/8oz/2 cups self-raising (self-rising) flour

15ml/1 tbsp baking powder

2.5ml/½ tsp salt

115g/4oz/½ cup butter, softened

200g/7oz/1 cup granulated sugar

2 eggs

5ml/1 tsp vanilla extract

175ml/6fl oz/¾ cup milk

For the filling

250ml/8fl oz/1 cup milk

3 egg yolks

90g/3½oz/½ cup granulated sugar

25g/1oz/¼ cup plain (all-purpose) flour

15g/½oz/1 tbsp butter

15ml/1 tbsp brandy or 5ml/1 tsp vanilla extract

For the chocolate glaze

25g/1oz cooking (unsweetened) chocolate

25g/1oz/2 tbsp butter or margarine

90g/3½oz/½ cup icing (confectioners') sugar, plus extra for dusting

2.5ml/½ tsp vanilla extract

about 15ml/1 tbsp hot water

1 Preheat the oven to 190°F/375°F/ Gas 5.

2 Grease two 20cm/8in shallow round cake tins (pans), and line the bottoms with greased baking parchment.

3 Sift the flour with the baking powder and salt.

4 Beat the butter and granulated sugar together until light and fluffy. Add the eggs one at a time, beating well after each addition. Stir in the vanilla. Add the milk and dry ingredients alternately, mixing only enough to blend thoroughly. Do not over-beat the mixture.

5 Divide the mixture between the prepared tins and spread it out evenly. Bake until a skewer inserted in the centre comes out clean, about 25 minutes.

6 Meanwhile, make the filling. Heat the milk in a small pan to boiling point. Remove from the heat.

7 ▲ In a heatproof mixing bowl, beat the egg yolks until smooth. Gradually add the granulated sugar and continue beating until pale yellow. Beat in the flour.

8 ▲ Pour the hot milk into the egg yolk mixture in a steady stream, beating constantly. When all the milk has been added, place the bowl over a pan of boiling water, or pour the mixture into the top of a double boiler. Heat, stirring constantly, until thickened. Cook for 2 minutes more, then remove from the heat. Stir in the butter and brandy or vanilla. Leave to cool.

9 ▲ When the cake layers have cooled, use a large sharp knife to slice off the domed top to make a flat surface. Place one layer on a serving plate and spread the filling on in a thick layer. Set the other layer on top, cut side down. Smooth the edge of the filling layer so it is flush with the sides of the cake layers.

10 ▲ For the glaze, melt the chocolate with the butter or margarine in the top of a double boiler, or in a bowl over hot water. When smooth, remove from the heat and beat in the sugar to make a thick paste. Add the vanilla. Beat in a little of the hot water. If the glaze does not have a spreadable consistency, add more water, 5ml/1 tsp at a time.

11 Spread the glaze evenly over the top of the cake, using a metal spatula. Dust the top with icing sugar. Because of the custard filling, any leftover cake must be chilled.

Shaker Summer Pudding

SERVES 6–8

1 loaf of white farmhouse-type bread,
  1–2 days old, sliced

675g/1½lb fresh redcurrants

50g/2oz/¼ cup plus 30ml/2 tbsp
  granulated sugar

50ml/2fl oz/¼ cup water

675g/1½lb berries: raspberries,
  blueberries and blackberries

juice of ½ lemon

whipped cream, to serve (optional)

1 ▲ Trim the crusts from the bread slices. Cut a round of bread to fit in the bottom of a 1.5 litre/2½ pint/6 cup domed pudding basin. Line the sides of the basin with bread slices, cutting them to fit and overlapping them slightly. Reserve enough bread slices to cover the top of the basin.

2 Combine the redcurrants with the 50g/2oz/¼ cup of sugar and the water in a non-metallic pan. Heat gently, crushing the berries lightly to help the juices flow. When the sugar has dissolved, remove from the heat.

3 Tip the currant mixture into a food processor or blender and process until quite smooth. Press through a fine-mesh nylon strainer set over a bowl. Discard the fruit pulp left in the strainer.

4 Put the berries in a bowl with the remaining sugar and the lemon juice. Stir well.

5 One at a time, remove the cut bread pieces from the basin and dip in the redcurrant purée. Replace to line the basin evenly.

6 ▲ Spoon the berries into the lined basin, pressing them down evenly. Top with the reserved cut bread slices, which have been dipped in the redcurrant purée.

7 Cover the basin with clear film (plastic wrap). Set a small plate, just big enough to fit inside the rim of the basin, on top of the pudding. Weigh it down with cans of food. Chill for 8–24 hours.

8 To turn the pudding out, remove the weights, plate and clear film. Run a knife between the basin and the pudding to loosen it. Turn out on to a serving plate. Serve in wedges, with whipped cream if you wish.

Apple Brown Betty

SERVES 6

50g/2oz/1 cup fresh breadcrumbs

150g/5oz/¾ cup soft light brown sugar

2.5ml/½ tsp ground cinnamon

1.5ml/¼ tsp ground cloves

1.5ml/¼ tsp grated nutmeg

50g/2oz/¼ cup butter

900g/2lb tart-sweet apples

juice of 1 lemon

40g/1½oz/⅓ cup finely chopped walnuts

1 Preheat the grill (broiler).

2 ▲ Spread the breadcrumbs on a baking sheet and toast under the grill until golden, stirring so they colour evenly. Set aside.

3 Preheat the oven to 190°C/375°F/Gas 5. Grease a 2.5 litre/4 pint baking dish.

4 ▲ Mix the sugar with the spices. Cut the butter into pea-size pieces; set aside.

5 ▲ Peel, core and slice the apples. Toss immediately with the lemon juice to prevent the apple slices from turning brown.

6 Sprinkle about 37ml/2½ tbsp breadcrumbs over the bottom of the prepared dish. Cover with one-third of the apples and sprinkle with one-third of the sugar-spice mixture. Add another layer of breadcrumbs and dot with one-third of the butter. Repeat the layers two more times, ending with a layer of breadcrumbs. Sprinkle with the nuts, and dot with the remaining butter.

7 Bake until the apples are tender and the top is golden brown, 35–40 minutes. Serve warm. It is good with cream or ice cream.

Maryland Peach and Blueberry Pie

SERVES 8

225g/8oz/2 cups plain (all-purpose) flour

2.5ml/½ tsp salt

5ml/1 tsp granulated sugar

150g/5oz/10 tbsp cold butter
  or margarine, diced

1 egg yolk

30–45ml/2–3 tbsp iced water

30ml/2 tbsp milk, for glazing

FOR THE FILLING

6 peaches, peeled, stoned and sliced

225g/8oz/2 cups fresh blueberries

150g/5oz/¾ cup granulated sugar

30ml/2 tbsp fresh lemon juice

40g/1½oz/⅓ cup plain (all-purpose) flour

pinch of grated nutmeg

25g/1oz/2 tbsp butter or margarine, cut
  into pea-size pieces

1 For the pastry, sift the flour, salt and sugar into a bowl. Using your fingertips, rub the butter or margarine into the dry ingredients as quickly as possible until the mixture is crumbly and resembles breadcrumbs.

2 Mix the egg yolk with 30ml/2 tbsp of the iced water and sprinkle over the flour mixture. Combine with a fork until the pastry holds together. If the pastry is too crumbly, add a little more water, 5ml/1 tsp at a time. Gather the pastry into a ball and flatten into a disk. Wrap in clear film (plastic wrap) and chill for at least 20 minutes.

3 Roll out two-thirds of the pastry between two sheets of baking parchment to a thickness of about 3mm/⅛in. Use to line a 23cm/9in tart tin (pan). Trim all around, leaving a 1cm/½in overhang. Fold the overhang under to form the edge. Using a fork, press the edge to the rim of the tin.

4 ▲ Gather the trimmings and remaining pastry into a ball, and roll out to a thickness of about 6mm/¼in. Using a pastry wheel or sharp knife, cut strips 1cm/½in wide. Chill the pastry case and the strips for 20 minutes.

5 Preheat the oven to 200°C/400°F/ Gas 6.

6 ▲ Line the pastry case with baking parchment and fill with dried beans. Bake until the pastry case is just set, 7–10 minutes. Remove from the oven and carefully lift out the paper with the beans. Prick the bottom of the pastry case all over with a fork, then return to the oven and bake for 5 minutes more. Let the pastry case cool slightly before filling. Leave the oven on.

7 ▲ In a mixing bowl, combine the peach slices with the blueberries, sugar, lemon juice, flour and nutmeg. Spoon the fruit mixture evenly into the pastry case. Dot with the pieces of butter or margarine.

8 ▲ Weave a lattice top with the chilled pastry strips, pressing the ends to the baked pastry-case edge. Brush the strips with the milk.

9 Bake the pie for 15 minutes. Reduce the heat to 180°C/350°F/Gas 4, and continue baking until the filling is tender and bubbling and the pastry lattice is golden, about 30 minutes more. If the pastry gets too brown, cover loosely with a piece of foil. Serve the pie warm or at room temperature.

Brethren's Cider Pie

Serves 6

175g/6oz/1½ cups plain (all-purpose) flour

1.5ml/¼ tsp salt

5ml/1 tsp caster (superfine) sugar

115g/4oz/½ cup cold butter or margarine, diced

30–45ml/3–4 tbsp iced water

For the filing

550ml/18fl oz/2½ cups cider

15ml/1 tbsp butter

250ml/8fl oz/1 cup maple syrup

50ml/2fl oz/¼ cup water

1.5ml/¼ tsp salt

2 eggs, at room temperature, separated

5ml/1 tsp grated nutmeg

1 ▲ For the pastry, sift the flour, salt and sugar into a bowl. With a pastry blender, cut in the butter until the mixture resembles breadcrumbs, or rub in with your fingertips.

2 Sprinkle 45ml/3 tbsp of the iced water over the flour mixture. Combine with a fork until the pastry holds together. If the pastry is too crumbly, add a little more water, 5ml/1 tsp at a time. Gather the pastry into a ball and flatten into a disk. Wrap in baking parchment and chill for 20 minutes.

3 ▲ Meanwhile, place the cider in a heavy pan. Boil until only 175ml/6fl oz/ ¾ cup remains. Leave to cool.

4 ▲ Roll out the pastry between two sheets of baking parchment to a thickness of about 3mm/⅛in. Use to line a 23cm/9in pie tin (pan).

5 ▲ Trim all around, leaving a 1cm/ ½in overhang. Fold the overhang under to form the edge. Using a fork, press the edge to the rim of the pan and press up from under with your fingers at intervals for a ruffle effect. Chill for 20 minutes.

6 Preheat the oven to 180°F/350°F/ Gas 4.

7 ▲ For the filling, add the butter, maple syrup, water and salt to the cider, bring to the boil and simmer gently for 5–6 minutes. Remove the pan from the heat and let the mixture cool slightly, then whisk in the beaten egg yolks.

8 ▲ In a large bowl, whisk the egg whites until they form stiff peaks. Add the cider mixture and fold gently together until evenly blended.

9 ▲ Pour into the prepared pastry case. Dust with the grated nutmeg.

10 Bake until the pastry is golden brown and the filling is well set, 30–35 minutes. Serve warm.

Vermont Baked Maple Custard

SERVES 6

3 eggs

185g/6½oz/½ cup maple syrup

550ml/18fl oz/2½ cups milk

pinch of salt

pinch of grated nutmeg

1 ▼ Preheat the oven to 180°F/
350°F/Gas 4. Combine all the
ingredients in a bowl and mix
together well.

2 ▲ Set individual ramekins in a
roasting pan half filled with hot water.
Pour the custard mixture into the
ramekins. Bake until the custards are
set, 45–60 minutes. Test by inserting
the blade of a knife in the centre; it
should come out clean. Serve warm
or chilled.

~ COOK'S TIP ~

Baking delicate mixtures such as
custards in a bain marie helps
protect them from uneven heating,
which could make them rubbery.

Cranberry Ice

MAKES ABOUT 1.75 LITRES/3 PINTS/7½ CUPS

2.5 litres/4 pints cranberries

475ml/16fl oz/2 cups water

350g/12oz/1¾ cups granulated sugar

1.5ml/¼ tsp grated orange rind

30ml/2 tbsp fresh orange juice

1 Check the manufacturer's
instructions for your ice cream maker,
if using one, to find out its capacity.
If necessary, halve the recipe.

2 ▲ Pick over and wash the
cranberries. Discard any that are
blemished or soft.

3 ▼ Place the cranberries in a non-
metallic pan with the water and bring
to the boil. Reduce the heat and
simmer until the cranberries are soft,
about 15 minutes.

4 Push the cranberry mixture through
a fine-mesh nylon strainer set over a
bowl. Return the purée to the pan,
add the sugar and stir to dissolve. Boil
for 5 minutes. Stir in the orange rind
and juice. Remove from the heat and
let the cranberry mixture cool down to
room temperature.

5 To freeze in an ice cream maker,
pour the cranberry mixture into the
machine and freeze following the
manufacturer's instructions.

6 ▲ If you do not have an ice cream
maker, pour the mixture into a metal
or plastic freezer container and freeze
until softly set, about 3 hours. Remove
the frozen cranberry mixture from the
container and chop roughly into 7.5cm/
3in pieces. Place in a food processor and
process until smooth. Return the mixture to the freezer container and freeze
again until firm. Repeat this freezing
and chopping process two or three
times, then leave to freeze until firm.

Vermont Baked Maple Custard (top), Cranberry Ice

THE SOUTH

RICH AND DIVERSE CULINARY
INFLUENCES – FRENCH, SPANISH,
NATIVE AMERICAN AND AFRICAN –
HAVE BROUGHT ABOUT SEVERAL
DISTINCT CUISINES, CAJUN BEING
PERHAPS THE MOST WELL KNOWN.
ALL HAVE CAPITALIZED ON THE
BOUNTY OF FIELD AND FOREST,
THE PROXIMITY OF WATER
THROUGHOUT MUCH OF THE
REGION AND A WARM CLIMATE.

Miami Chilled Avocado Soup

2 large or 3 medium ripe avocados

15ml/1 tbsp fresh lemon juice

75g/3oz/¾ cup coarsely chopped peeled cucumber

30ml/2 tbsp dry sherry

75g/3oz/¼ cup coarsely chopped spring onions (scallions), with some of the green stems

475ml/16fl oz/2 cups mild-flavoured chicken stock

5ml/1 tsp salt

hot pepper sauce (optional)

natural (plain) yogurt or cream, to serve

1 ▼ Halve the avocados, pull out the stones (pits) and peel. Roughly chop the flesh and place in a food processor or blender. Add the lemon juice and process until very smooth.

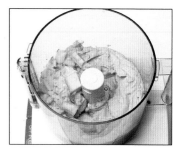

2 ▲ Add the cucumber, sherry and most of the spring onions. Process again until smooth.

3 ▲ In a large bowl, combine the avocado mixture with the chicken stock. Whisk until well blended. Season with the salt and a few drops of hot pepper sauce, if you like. Cover the bowl and chill well.

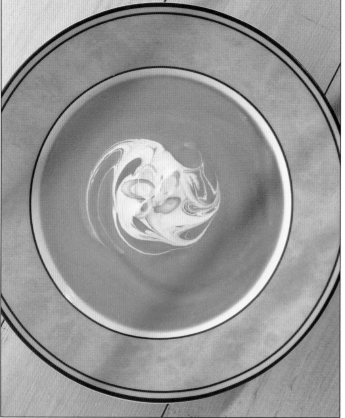

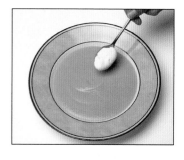

4 ▲ To serve, fill individual bowls with the soup. Place a spoonful of yogurt or cream in the centre of each bowl and swirl with a spoon. Sprinkle with the reserved spring onions.

Shrimp and Corn Bisque

SERVES 4

30ml/2 tbsp olive oil

1 onion, finely chopped

50g/2oz/¼ cup butter or margarine

25g/1oz/¼ cup plain (all-purpose) flour

750ml/1¼ pints/3 cups fish or chicken
   stock, or clam juice

250ml/8fl oz/1 cup milk

150g/5oz/1 cup peeled cooked small
   prawns, (shrimp), deveined if necessary

250g/9oz/1½ cups corn kernels (fresh,
   frozen or canned)

2.5ml/½ tsp finely chopped fresh dill
   or thyme

salt

hot pepper sauce

120ml/4fl oz/½ cup single (light) cream

1 Heat the olive oil in a large heavy
pan. Add the onion and cook over a a
low heat until softened, 8–10 minutes.

2 Meanwhile, melt the butter or
margarine in a medium heavy pan.
Add the flour and stir with a wire
whisk until blended. Cook for
1–2 minutes. Pour in the stock and
milk and stir to blend. Bring to the
boil over a medium heat and cook for
5–8 minutes, stirring frequently.

4 ▼ Add the sauce mixture to the
prawn and corn mixture and mix
well. Remove 750ml/1¼ pints/3 cups of
the soup and purée in a blender or food
processor. Return it to the rest of the
soup in the pan and stir well. Season
with salt and hot pepper sauce to taste.

5 ▲ Add the cream and stir to blend.
Heat the soup almost to boiling point,
stirring frequently. Serve hot.

3 ▲ Cut each prawn into two or three
pieces and add to the onion with the
corn and dill or thyme. Cook for
2–3 minutes, stirring occasionally.
Remove the pan from the heat.

Palm Beach Papaya and Avocado Salad

SERVES 4

2 ripe avocados

1 ripe papaya

1 large sweet orange

1 small red onion

115g/4oz/2 cups small rocket
  (arugula) leaves

FOR THE DRESSING

50ml/2fl oz/¼ cup olive oil

30ml/2 tbsp fresh lemon or lime juice

salt and pepper

1 ▼ Halve the avocados and remove
the stones (pits). Carefully peel off the
skin. Cut each avocado in half lengthways into four thick slices.

2 ▲ Peel the papaya. Cut it in half
lengthways and scoop out the seeds
with a spoon. Set aside 5ml/1 tsp of
the seeds for the dressing. Cut each
papaya half lengthways into eight slices.

3 ▲ Peel the orange. Using a sharp
paring knife, cut out the sections,
cutting on either side of the dividing
membranes. Cut the onion into very
thin slices and separate into rings.

4 ▲ Combine the dressing
ingredients in a bowl and mix well.
Stir in the reserved papaya seeds.

5 Assemble the salad on four
individual serving plates. Alternate
slices of papaya and avocado and add
the orange sections and a small mound
of rocket topped with onion rings.
Spoon on the dressing.

Warm Salad of Black-eyed Beans

SERVES 4

2 small red (bell) peppers

2.5ml/½ tsp Dijon-style mustard

30ml/2 tbsp wine vinegar

1.5ml/¼ tsp salt

pinch of pepper

90ml/6 tbsp olive oil

30ml/2 tbsp finely chopped fresh chives

350g/12oz/3 cups fresh black-eyed
    beans (peas)

1 bay leaf

8 lean bacon rashers (strips)

1 Preheat the grill (broiler).

2 ▲ Grill (broil) the peppers until the
skins blacken and blister, turning the
peppers so that all sides are charred.
Remove from the grill and place
the peppers in a paper or plastic bag
to steam. Leave to cool for 10 minutes.

3 Peel off the skins. Cut the peppers in
half, discard the seeds, white membranes
and stem, and slice into 1 × 5cm/½ ×
2in strips. Set aside.

~ COOK'S TIP ~

If preferred, chop the roasted red
(bell) peppers rather than cutting
them into strips and mix into the
warm black-eyed beans (peas).

4 ▼ Combine the mustard and
vinegar in a small bowl. Add the salt
and pepper. Beat in the oil until well
blended. Add the chives.

5 Add the black-eyed beans to a pan of
boiling salted water, with the bay leaf.
Boil until just tender, 13–15 minutes.

6 Meanwhile, cook the bacon until
crisp. Drain on kitchen paper. Cut or
break into small pieces.

7 ▲ When the black-eyed beans are
done, drain them and discard the bay
leaf. While they are still warm, toss
them with the chive dressing.

8 Make a mound of beans on a serving
dish. Sprinkle with the bacon pieces
and garnish with the strips of red
pepper. Serve warm.

Fromajardis

MAKES ABOUT 40

225g/8oz/2 cups plain (all-purpose) flour
1.5ml/¼ tsp grated nutmeg
2.5ml/½ tsp salt
150g/5oz/10 tbsp cold butter, lard or white cooking fat, diced
45–60ml/4–5 tbsp iced water
FOR THE FILLING
2 eggs
115g/4oz mature (sharp) Cheddar cheese, grated
hot pepper sauce, to taste
15ml/1 tbsp finely chopped mixed fresh herbs, such as thyme, chives and sage

1 For the pastry, sift the flour, nutmeg and salt into a bowl. Using your fingertips, rub the butter, lard or white cooking fat into the dry ingredients as quickly as possible until the mixture is crumbly and resembles breadcrumbs.

2 ▲ Sprinkle 60ml/4 tbsp of the iced water over the flour mixture. Combine with a fork until the pastry holds together. If the pastry is too crumbly, add a little more water, 5ml/1 tsp at a time. Gather the pastry into a ball.

3 ▲ Divide the pastry in half and pat each portion into a disk. Wrap in clear film (plastic wrap); chill for 20 minutes.

4 Preheat the oven to 220°C/425°F/Gas 7.

5 ▲ For the filling, put the eggs in a mixing bowl and beat well with a fork. Add the cheese, hot pepper sauce to taste and the herbs.

6 ▲ On a lightly floured surface, roll out the dough to a thickness of 3mm/⅛in or less. Cut out rounds using a 7.5cm/3in drinking glass or cutter.

7 ▲ Place 5ml/1 tsp of the filling in the centre of each pastry round. Fold over to make half-moon shapes, and press the edges together with the tines of a fork. A bit of filling may ooze through the seam.

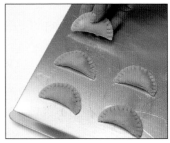

8 ▲ Cut a few small slashes in the top of each pastry with the point of a sharp knife. Place on ungreased baking sheets. Bake until the pastries start to darken slightly, 18–20 minutes. To test if they are cooked, cut one in half; the pastry should be cooked through. Serve warm with drinks.

~ COOK'S TIP ~

The fromajardis may be made ahead of time. Leave them to cool on a wire rack and then store in an airtight container. Just before serving, reheat the pastries in a preheated 190°C/375°F/Gas 5 oven for 5–10 minutes.

Crab Bayou

SERVES 6

450g/1lb fresh crab meat

3 hard-boiled egg yolks

5ml/1 tsp Dijon-style mustard

75g/3oz/6 tbsp butter or margarine,
at room temperature

1.5ml/¼ tsp cayenne pepper

45ml/3 tbsp sherry

30ml/2 tbsp finely chopped fresh parsley

120ml/4fl oz/½ cup whipping cream

50g/2oz/½ cup thinly sliced spring onions
(scallions), including some of the
green stems

salt and black pepper

30g/1¼oz/½ cup dried breadcrumbs

1 Preheat oven to 180°C/350°F/Gas 4.

2 ▼ Pick over the crab meat and
remove any shell or cartilage, keeping
the pieces of crab as big as possible.

3 ▲ In a medium bowl, crumble the
egg yolks with a fork. Add the
mustard, 60ml/4 tbsp of the butter or
margarine, and the cayenne, and
mash together to form a paste. Mash
in the sherry and parsley.

4 ▲ Mix in the cream and spring
onions. Stir in the crab meat. Season
with salt and pepper.

5 ▲ Divide the mixture equally among
six greased scallop shells or other
individual baking dishes. Sprinkle with
the breadcrumbs and dot with the
remaining butter or margarine.

6 Bake until bubbling hot and golden
brown, about 20 minutes.

Cajun "Popcorn" with Basil Mayonnaise

SERVES 8

900g/2lb raw crayfish tails, peeled, or small prawns (shrimp), peeled and deveined

2 eggs

250ml/8fl oz/1 cup dry white wine

50g/2oz/½ cup fine cornmeal, or plain (all-purpose) flour if not available

50g/2oz/½ cup plain flour

15ml/1 tbsp finely chopped fresh chives

1 garlic clove, finely chopped

2.5ml/½ tsp fresh thyme leaves

1.5ml/¼ tsp salt

1.5ml/¼ tsp cayenne pepper

1.5ml/¼ tsp black pepper

oil for deep-frying

FOR THE MAYONNAISE

1 egg yolk

10ml/2 tsp Dijon-style mustard

15ml/1 tbsp white wine vinegar

salt and pepper

250ml/8fl oz/1 cup olive or vegetable oil

25g/1oz/½ cup finely chopped fresh basil leaves

1 ▲ Rinse the crayfish tails or prawns in cool water. Drain well and set aside in a cool place.

2 Mix together the eggs and wine in a small bowl.

3 ▼ In a mixing bowl, combine the cornmeal and/or flour, chives, garlic, thyme, salt, cayenne and pepper. Gradually whisk in the egg mixture, blending well. Cover the batter and leave to stand for 1 hour.

4 For the mayonnaise, combine the egg yolk, mustard and vinegar in a mixing bowl. Add salt and pepper to taste. Add the oil in a thin stream, beating vigorously with a wire whisk. When the mixture is thick and smooth, stir in the basil. Cover and chill until ready to serve.

5 Heat 5–7.5cm/2–3in oil in a large frying pan or deep-fryer to 188–190°C/365–370°F. Dip the seafood into the batter and fry in small batches until golden brown, 2–3 minutes. Turn as necessary for even colouring. Remove with a slotted spoon and drain on kitchen paper. Serve hot, with the basil mayonnaise.

Crayfish or Prawn Etouffée

SERVES 6

1.2kg/2½lb raw crayfish or prawns
  (shrimp) in shell

750ml/1¼ pints/3 cups water

75ml/2½ fl oz/⅓ cup vegetable oil or lard

40g/1½oz/⅓ cup plain (all-purpose) flour

1½ onions, finely chopped

50g/2oz/¼ cup finely chopped green
  (bell) pepper

25g/1oz/¼ cup finely chopped celery

1 garlic clove, finely chopped

120ml/4fl oz/½ cup dry white wine

25g/1oz/2 tbsp butter or margarine

25g/1oz/½ cup finely chopped
  fresh parsley

15g/½oz/¼ cup finely chopped
  fresh chives

salt

hot pepper sauce

rice, to serve

1 ▲ Peel and devein the crayfish or
prawns; reserve the heads and shells.
Keep the seafood in a covered bowl in
the refrigerator; put the heads and
shells in a large pot with the water.

2 Bring the pot to the boil, cover and
simmer for 15 minutes. Strain and
reserve 350ml/12fl oz/1½ cups of this
stock. Set aside.

3 To make the Cajun roux, heat the
oil or lard in a heavy cast iron frying
pan or steel pan.

4 ▲ When the oil is hot, add the
flour, a little at a time, and blend to a
smooth paste using a long-handled
flat-bottomed wooden spoon.

5 ▲ Cook over a medium-low heat,
stirring constantly, until the Cajun
roux reaches the desired colour,
25–40 minutes. It will gradually deepen
in colour from light beige to tan, to a
deeper, redder brown. When it reaches
the colour of peanut butter, remove
the pan from the heat and immediately
mix in the onions, pepper and celery.
Continue stirring to prevent any
further darkening.

6 ▲ Return the pan to a low heat. Add
the garlic and cook for 1–2 minutes,
stirring. Add the seafood stock and
blend well with a wire whisk. Whisk
in the white wine.

7 ▲ Bring to the boil, stirring,
and simmer until the sauce is thick,
3–4 minutes. Remove from the heat.

8 ▲ In a large heavy pan, melt the
butter or margarine. Add the crayfish
or prawns, stir and cook until pink,
2–3 minutes. Stir in the parsley
and chives.

9 Add the sauce and stir well to
combine. Season with salt and hot
pepper sauce to taste. Simmer over a
medium heat for 3–4 minutes more.
Serve hot with rice.

~ COOK'S TIP ~

When making the Cajun roux,
take great care not to burn the
flour. If the mixture starts to
smoke, immediately remove the
pan from the heat and stir until
the mixture cools slightly. If the
flour mixture should burn, or if
black specks appear, throw it away
and start again, or the étouffée
will have a bitter burned taste.
Do not use a nonstick pan.

Prawn-stuffed Aubergines

SERVES 4

2 large firm aubergines (eggplants)

30ml/2 tbsp fresh lemon juice

40g/1½oz/3 tbsp butter or margarine

225g/8oz raw prawns (shrimp), peeled
  and deveined

40g/1½oz/½ cup thinly sliced spring onions
  (scallions), including some green stems

350g/12oz/1½ cups chopped
  fresh tomatoes

1 garlic clove, finely chopped

15g/½oz/¼ cup chopped fresh parsley

15g/½oz/¼ cup chopped fresh basil

pinch of grated nutmeg

salt and pepper

hot pepper sauce, to taste

30g/1¼oz/½ cup dried breadcrumbs

rice, to serve (optional)

1 Preheat oven to 190°C/375°F/Gas 5.

2 ▲ Cut the aubergines in half
lengthways. With a small sharp knife,
cut around the inside edge of each
aubergine half, about 1cm/½in from
the skin. Carefully scoop out the flesh,
leaving a shell 1cm/½in thick.

3 Immerse the shells, skin side up,
in cold water to prevent them from
discolouring.

~ COOK'S TIP ~

This can also be served cold
for an unusual summer dish.

4 ▲ Chop the scooped-out aubergine
flesh coarsely, toss with the lemon
juice and set aside.

5 ▲ Melt 25g/1oz/2 tbsp of the butter
or margarine in a frying pan. Add
the prawns and sauté until pink,
2–3 minutes, turning so they cook
evenly. Remove the prawns with a
slotted spoon and set aside.

6 ▲ Add the spring onions to the pan
and cook over a medium heat for about
2 minutes, stirring constantly. Add
the tomatoes, garlic and parsley and
cook for 5 minutes more.

7 Add the chopped aubergines, basil and
nutmeg. If necessary, add a little water
to prevent the vegetables sticking.
Mix well. Cover and simmer for
8–10 minutes. Remove from the heat.

8 ▲ Cut each prawn into two or three
pieces. Stir into the vegetable mixture.
Season with salt, pepper and hot pepper
sauce to taste.

9 Lightly oil a shallow baking tin (pan)
large enough to hold the aubergine
halves in one layer. Drain and dry the
aubergine shells and arrange in the pan.

10 ▲ Sprinkle a layer of breadcrumbs
into each shell. Spoon in a layer of the
prawn mixture. Repeat, finishing with
a layer of breadcrumbs.

11 ▲ Dot with the remaining butter
or margarine. Bake until bubbling hot
and golden brown on top, about
20–25 minutes. Serve immediately,
accompanied by rice, if you wish.

Prawns Creole

SERVES 4

675g/1½lb raw prawns (shrimp) in shell, with heads, if available

475ml/16fl oz/2 cups water

45ml/3 tbsp olive or vegetable oil

3 onions, finely chopped

50g/2oz/½ cup finely chopped celery

115g/4oz/½ cup finely chopped green (bell) pepper

25g/1oz/½ cup chopped fresh parsley

1 garlic clove, finely chopped

15ml/1 tbsp Worcestershire sauce

1.5ml/¼ tsp cayenne pepper

120ml/4fl oz/½ cup dry white wine

225g/8oz/1 cup chopped peeled plum tomatoes

5ml/1 tsp salt

1 bay leaf

5ml/1 tsp granulated sugar

rice, to serve

1 ▲ Peel and devein the prawns; reserve the heads and shells. Keep the prawns in a covered bowl in the refrigerator while you make the sauce.

2 Put the prawn heads and shells in a pan with the water. Bring to the boil and simmer for 15 minutes. Strain and reserve 350ml/2fl oz/1½ cups of this stock. Set the stock aside.

3 ▲ Heat the oil in a heavy pan. Add the onions and cook over a low heat until softened, 8–10 minutes. Add the celery and pepper and cook for 5 minutes more. Stir in the parsley, garlic, Worcestershire sauce and cayenne. Cook for another 5 minutes, stirring occasionally.

4 Raise the heat to medium. Stir in the wine and simmer for 3–4 minutes. Add the tomatoes, prawns, stock, salt, bay leaf and sugar and bring to the boil. Stir well, then reduce the heat to low and simmer until the tomatoes have fallen apart and the sauce has reduced slightly, about 30 minutes. Remove from the heat and leave to cool slightly.

5 Discard the bay leaf. Pour the sauce into a food processor or blender and process until quite smooth. Taste and adjust the seasoning.

6 ▲ Return the sauce to the pan and bring to the boil. Add the prawns and simmer until they turn pink, 4–5 minutes only. Serve with rice.

Fried Catfish Fillets with Piquant Sauce

SERVES 4

1 egg

50ml/2fl oz/¼ cup olive oil

squeeze of lemon juice

2.5ml/½ tsp finely chopped fresh dill or parsley

salt and pepper

4 catfish fillets

50g/2oz/½ cup plain (all-purpose) flour

25g/1oz/2 tbsp butter or margarine

FOR THE SAUCE

1 egg yolk

30ml/2 tbsp Dijon-style mustard

30ml/2 tbsp white wine vinegar

10ml/2 tsp paprika

300ml/½ pint/1¼ cups olive or vegetable oil

30ml/2 tbsp prepared horseradish

2.5ml/½ tsp finely chopped garlic

25g/1oz/¼ cup finely chopped celery

30ml/2 tbsp tomato ketchup

2.5ml/½ tsp pepper

2.5ml/½ tsp salt

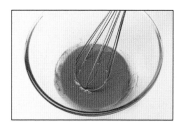

1 ▲ For the sauce, combine the egg yolk, mustard, vinegar and paprika in a mixing bowl. Add the oil in a thin stream, beating vigorously with a wire whisk to blend it in.

~ VARIATION ~

If preferred, serve the catfish fillets with lime or lemon wedges.

2 ▲ When the mixture is smooth and thick, beat in all the other sauce ingredients. Cover and chill until ready to serve.

3 ▲ Combine the egg, 15ml/1 tbsp of the olive oil, the lemon juice, herbs and a little salt and pepper in a shallow dish. Beat until well combined.

4 ▼ Dip both sides of each catfish fillet in the egg and herb mixture, then coat lightly with flour, shaking off the excess.

5 Heat the butter or margarine with the remaining olive oil in a large heavy frying pan. Add the fillets and fry until golden brown on both sides and cooked, 8–10 minutes. To test if it is done, insert the point of a sharp knife into the fish: it should still be just opaque in the centre.

6 Serve the catfish fillets hot, with the piquant sauce.

Seafood and Sausage Gumbo

SERVES 10–12

1.3kg/3lb raw prawns (shrimp) in shell, with heads, if available

1.65 litres/2¾ pints/7 cups water

1 onion, quartered

4 bay leaves

175ml/6fl oz/¾ cup vegetable oil

115g/4oz/1 cup plain (all-purpose) flour

50g/2oz/¼ cup margarine or butter

6 onions, finely chopped

450g/1lb/2 cups finely chopped green (bell) pepper

225g/8oz/2 cups finely chopped celery

675g/1½lb kielbasa (Polish) or andouille sausage, cut into 1cm/½in rounds

450g/1lb fresh okra, cut into 1cm/½in slices

3 garlic cloves, finely chopped

2.5ml/½ tsp fresh or dried thyme leaves

10ml/2 tsp salt

2.5ml/½ tsp black pepper

2.5ml/½ tsp white pepper

5ml/1 tsp cayenne pepper

hot pepper sauce (optional)

450g/1lb/2 cups chopped peeled fresh or canned plum tomatoes

450g/1lb fresh crab meat

rice, to serve

1 Peel and devein the prawns; reserve the heads and shells. Keep the prawns in a covered bowl in the refrigerator while you make the sauce.

2 Put the prawn heads and shells in a pan with the water, quartered onion and one of the bay leaves. Bring to the boil, then partly cover and simmer for 20 minutes. Strain and set aside.

3 Heat the oil in a heavy cast iron or steel pan. (Do not use a non-stick pan.) When the oil is hot, add the flour, a little at a time, and blend to a smooth paste using a long-handled flat-bottomed wooden spoon.

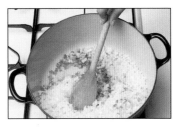

4 ▲ Cook over a medium-low heat, stirring constantly, until the Cajun roux reaches the desired colour, about 25–40 minutes. The roux will gradually deepen in colour from light beige to tan, to a deeper, redder brown. When it reaches the colour of peanut butter, remove the pan from the heat and continue stirring until the roux has cooled and stopped cooking.

5 ▲ Melt the margarine or butter in a large heavy pan. Add the finely chopped onions, bell pepper and celery. Cook over a medium-low heat until the onions are softened, 6–8 minutes, stirring occasionally.

6 ▲ Add the sausage and mix well. Cook for 5 minutes more. Add the okra and garlic, stir and cook until the okra stops producing white "threads".

7 ▲ Add the remaining bay leaves, the thyme, salt, both peppers, cayenne and hot pepper sauce to taste, if you like. Mix well. Stir in 1.3 litres/2¼ pints/ 6 cups of the prawn stock and the tomatoes. Bring to the boil, then partly cover the pan, lower the heat and simmer for about 20 minutes.

8 Whisk in the Cajun roux. Raise the heat and bring to the boil, whisking well. Lower the heat again and simmer, uncovered, for 40–50 minutes more, stirring occasionally.

9 ▲ Gently stir in the prawns and crabmeat. Cook until the prawns turn pink, 3–4 minutes. To serve, put a mound of hot rice in each serving bowl and ladle on the gumbo, making sure each person gets some seafood and some sausage.

~ COOK'S TIP ~

Heavy pans retain their heat. When making a Cajun roux, do not let it get too dark, as the roux will continue cooking off the heat.

Smothered Rabbit

SERVES 4

90ml/6 tbsp soy sauce

hot pepper sauce, to taste

2.5ml/½ tsp white pepper

5ml/1 tsp sweet paprika

5ml/1 tsp dried basil

0.9–1.3kg/2–3lb rabbit, cut into pieces

45ml/3 tbsp peanut or olive oil

90g/3½oz/¾ cup plain (all-purpose) flour

4 onions, finely sliced

250ml/8fl oz/1 cup dry white wine

250ml/8fl oz/1 cup chicken or meat stock

5ml/1 tsp salt

5ml/1 tsp finely chopped garlic

25g/1oz/½ cup finely chopped fresh parsley

mashed potatoes or rice, to serve

1 ▼ Combine the soy sauce, hot pepper sauce to taste, white pepper, paprika and basil in a medium bowl. Add the rabbit pieces and rub them with the mixture. Leave to marinate for at least 1 hour.

2 ▲ Heat the oil in a high-sided ovenproof frying pan or large saucepan. Coat the rabbit pieces lightly in the flour, shaking off the excess. Brown the rabbit in the hot oil, turning frequently, for 5–6 minutes. Remove and set aside.

3 Preheat the oven to 180°F/350°F/Gas 4.

4 ▲ Add the onions to the pan and cook over a low heat until softened, 8–10 minutes. Raise the heat to medium, add the wine and stir well to mix in all the cooking juices.

5 Return the rabbit to the pan. Add the stock, salt, garlic and parsley. Mix well and turn the rabbit to coat with the sauce.

6 Cover the frying pan and place it in the oven. Cook until the rabbit is tender, about 1 hour, stirring occasionally. Serve with mashed potatoes or rice.

Pork Jambalaya

SERVES 6

1.2kg/2½lb boneless pork shoulder

50ml/2fl oz/¼ cup olive oil

3 onions, finely chopped

115g/4oz/1 cup finely chopped celery

350g/12oz/1½ cups finely chopped green or red (bell) peppers

250g/9oz/1½ cups smoked ham, such as tasso, cut into 1cm/½in cubes

5ml/1 tsp black pepper

5ml/1 tsp white pepper

2.5ml/½ tsp cayenne

5ml/1 tsp salt

1 garlic clove, finely chopped

350g/12oz/1½ cups chopped peeled fresh or canned tomatoes

1 bay leaf

2.5ml/½ tsp fresh or dried thyme leaves

hot pepper sauce

250ml/8fl oz/1 cup dry white wine

400g/14oz/2 cups long-grain rice

0.75–1 litre/1¼–1¾ pints/3–4 cups chicken stock, heated

1 Remove any visible fat or gristle from the pork, and cut the meat into 1cm/½in cubes.

2 ▲ Heat the oil in a large casserole or pan. Brown the cubes of pork, in batches, stirring to colour evenly. Remove the pork with a slotted spoon and set aside.

3 ▼ Add the onions, celery and peppers to the casserole and cook, stirring, for 3–4 minutes. Add the ham, black and white peppers, cayenne and salt. Cook over a medium heat, stirring frequently, until the onions are soft and golden, about 12 minutes.

4 Add the garlic, tomatoes, herbs and hot pepper sauce to taste. Cook for 5 minutes more. Add the pork and wine and mix well, then cover the casserole and cook gently over a low heat for about 45 minutes.

5 Add the rice and stir well. Cook for 3–4 minutes.

6 Pour in 750ml/1¼ pints/3 cups of the chicken stock and stir to blend. Bring to the boil. Cover, reduce the heat to low and simmer until the rice is tender, about 15 minutes. Stir the mixture occasionally and add more chicken stock if necessary. The rice should be moist, not dry and fluffy. Serve straight from the casserole or in a large heated serving dish.

Pecan-stuffed Pork Chops

SERVES 4

4 pork chops, at least 2.5cm/1in thick,
  trimmed of almost all fat

25g/1oz/½ cup fresh breadcrumbs

40g/1½oz/½ cup finely chopped spring
  onions (scallions)

1 apple, finely chopped

50g/2oz/½ cup chopped pecans

1 garlic clove, finely chopped

15g/½oz/¼ cup finely chopped
  fresh parsley

1.5ml/¼ tsp cayenne

1.5ml/¼ tsp black pepper

2.5ml/½ tsp dry mustard

pinch of ground cumin

30ml/2 tbsp olive oil

120ml/4fl oz/½ cup meat or chicken stock

120ml/4fl oz/½ cup dry white wine

1 bay leaf

1 Preheat the oven to 180°F/350°F/
Gas 4.

2 ▲ Make a pocket in each chop by
cutting horizontally from the fatty side
straight to the bone.

3 ▲ Combine all the other ingredients
except the stock, wine and bay leaf.
Mix well. Divide the mixture among the
chops, filling each pocket with as much
stuffing as it will comfortably hold.

4 ▲ Place the chops in a greased
baking dish large enough to hold them
in one layer.

5 ▲ Pour the stock and wine over
them and add the bay leaf and any
leftover stuffing. Cover tightly. Bake
until tender, about 1 hour, basting
occasionally with the pan juices. Serve
with the cooking juices spooned over.

Ham with Red-eye Gravy

SERVES 1

15ml/1 tbsp butter or margarine

1 slice of ham, 5–10mm/¼–½in thick,
  preferably uncooked country-style
  ham, with some fat left on it

120ml/4fl oz/½ cup strong coffee, heated

mashed potatoes, to serve (optional)

~ COOK'S TIP ~

Try ham cooked this way for
breakfast, accompanied by grits.

1 ▼ Melt the butter or margarine in
a small frying pan. Add the ham and
sauté until golden brown on both sides.
Remove to a warm plate.

2 ▲ Pour the coffee into the pan and
stir to mix with the cooking juices.
When the gravy is boiling, pour it over
the ham. Serve the ham with mashed
potatoes, if you like.

Pecan-stuffed Pork Chops (top), Ham with Red-Eye Gravy

Oven "Fried" Chicken

SERVES 4

4 large chicken pieces

50g/2oz/½ cup plain (all-purpose) flour

2.5ml/½ tsp salt

1.5ml/¼ tsp pepper

1 egg

30ml/2 tbsp water

30ml/2 tbsp finely chopped mixed fresh
herbs, such as parsley, basil and thyme

65g/2½oz/1 cup dried breadcrumbs

20g/¾oz/¼ cup freshly grated
Parmesan cheese

lemon wedges, to garnish

1 Preheat the oven to 200°C/400°F/
Gas 6. Rinse the chicken pieces in
cool water. Pat dry with kitchen paper.

2 ▼ Combine the flour, salt and
pepper on a plate and stir with a fork
to mix. Coat the chicken pieces on
both sides with the seasoned flour and
shake off the excess.

3 Sprinkle a little water on to the
chicken pieces, and coat again lightly
with the seasoned flour.

4 ▲ Beat the egg with the water in a
shallow dish. Stir in the herbs. Dip
the chicken pieces into the egg
mixture, turning to coat them evenly.

5 ▲ Combine the breadcrumbs and
the grated Parmesan cheese on a plate.
Roll the chicken pieces in the crumbs,
patting with your fingers to help them
to stick.

6 ▲ Place the chicken pieces in a
greased shallow pan large enough to
hold them in one layer. Bake until
thoroughly cooked and golden brown,
20–30 minutes. To test if they are
done, prick with a fork; the juices that
run out should be clear, not pink.
Serve hot, with lemon wedges.

Blackened Chicken Breasts

SERVES 6

6 medium-size skinless chicken
  breast fillets

75g/3oz/6 tbsp butter or margarine

5ml/1 tsp garlic powder

10ml/2 tsp onion powder

5ml/1 tsp cayenne pepper

10ml/2 tsp sweet paprika

7.5ml/1½ tsp salt

2.5ml/½ tsp white pepper

5ml/1 tsp black pepper

1.5ml/¼ tsp ground cumin

5ml/1 tsp dried thyme leaves

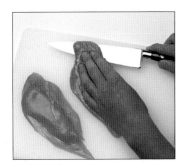

1 ▲ Slice each chicken piece in half
horizontally, making two pieces of
about the same thickness. Flatten
slightly with the heel of the hand.

2 Melt the butter or margarine in a
small pan.

~ VARIATION ~

For Blackened Catfish Fillets,
substitute six medium catfish fillets
for the chicken. Do not slice them
in half, but season as chicken and
cook for 2 minutes on the first side
and 1½–2 minutes on the other,
or until the fish flakes easily.

3 ▼ Combine all the remaining
ingredients in a shallow bowl and stir
to blend well. Brush the chicken
pieces on both sides with melted
butter or margarine, then sprinkle
evenly with the seasoning mixture.

4 Heat a large heavy frying pan over
high heat until a drop of water
sprinkled on the surface sizzles.
This will take 5–8 minutes.

5 ▲ Drizzle 5ml/1 tsp melted butter
on each chicken piece. Place them in
the frying pan in an even layer, two or
three at a time. Cook until the underside
begins to blacken, 2–3 minutes. Turn
and cook the other side for 2–3 minutes
more. Serve hot.

Corn Maque Choux

SERVES 4

30ml/2 tbsp groundnut (peanut) or
  olive oil

1 onion, finely chopped

40g/1½oz/⅓ cup finely chopped celery

65g/2½oz/⅓ cup finely chopped
  red (bell) pepper

475g/18oz/3 cups corn kernels (fresh,
  frozen or canned)

2.5ml/½ tsp cayenne pepper

120ml/4fl oz/½ cup dry white wine
  or water

1 medium tomato, diced

5ml/1 tsp salt

black pepper

45ml/3 tbsp whipping cream

30ml/2 tbsp shredded fresh basil

1 Heat the oil in a heavy frying
pan. Add the onion and cook over
a low heat until softened, about
8–10 minutes, stirring occasionally.

2 ▲ Raise the heat to medium, add
the celery and pepper and cook for
5 minutes more, stirring.

3 ▲ Stir in the corn kernels and the
cayenne pepper and cook until the
corn begins to stick to the bottom of
the pan, about 10 minutes.

4 ▲ Pour in the wine or water and
scrape up the corn from the bottom of
the pan. Add the tomato, salt and
pepper to taste. Mix well. Cover and
cook over a low heat until the tomato
has softened, 8–10 minutes.

5 ▲ Remove from the heat, stir in
the cream and basil and serve.

Spring Greens and Rice

SERVES 4

475ml/16fl oz/2 cups chicken or
  meat stock

200g/7oz/1 cup long grain rice

15ml/1 tbsp butter or margarine

2.5ml/½ tsp salt

175g/6oz/3 cups chopped spring greens
  (collard leaves), loosely packed

pepper

1 ▼ Bring the stock to the boil in a
medium pan. Add the rice, butter or
margarine and salt. Stir.

2 ▲ Add the greens, a handful at a
time, stirring well after each addition.

3 Bring back to the boil, then cover,
reduce the heat and cook until the rice
is tender, 15–20 minutes. Season with
pepper before serving.

Corn Maque Choux (top), Spring Greens and Rice

Dirty Rice

SERVES 4

90ml/6 tbsp olive or vegetable oil

2 onions, finely chopped

225g/8oz pork mince

1 garlic clove, finely chopped

225g/8oz chicken gizzards, chopped

50g/2oz/½ cup finely chopped celery

115g/4oz/½ cup finely chopped red or
    green (bell) pepper

2.5ml/½ tsp white pepper

5ml/1 tsp cayenne

1 bay leaf

2.5ml/½ tsp fresh or dried thyme leaves

5ml/1 tsp salt

750ml/1¼ pints/3 cups chicken stock

225g/8oz chicken livers, chopped

200g/7oz/1 cup long grain rice

45ml/3 tbsp chopped fresh parsley

1 Heat the oil in a large frying pan over a low heat. Add the onion and cook until softened, 8–10 minutes.

2 ▼ Add the pork mince. Raise the heat to medium-high and stir with a fork or wooden spoon to break up the lumps. When the meat has lost its pink, raw colour, add the garlic and gizzards. Stir well. Cover the pan, lower the heat to medium and cook for about 10 minutes, stirring occasionally.

3 ▲ Add the celery and pepper and cook for 5 minutes more. Stir in the white pepper, cayenne, bay leaf, thyme and salt. Add the chicken stock, stirring to scrape up the cooking juices in the bottom of the frying pan. Cook for about 10 minutes, stirring occasionally.

4 ▲ Add the chicken livers and cook for 2 minutes, stirring.

5 ▲ Stir in the rice. Reduce the heat to low, cover the pan, and cook until the rice is tender, 15–20 minutes. Stir in the parsley before serving.

Spoonbread

SERVES 4

550ml/18fl oz/2½ cups milk
115g/4oz/1 cup yellow cornmeal
75g/3oz/6 tbsp butter or margarine
5ml/1 tsp salt
7.5ml/1½ tsp baking powder
3 eggs, separated

1 Preheat the oven to 190°C/375°F/ Gas 5.

2 ▲ Heat the milk in a heavy pan. Just before it boils, beat in the cornmeal with a wire whisk. Cook over a low heat for about 10 minutes, stirring constantly.

3 ▲ Remove from the heat and beat in the butter or margarine, salt and baking powder.

4 ▼ Add the egg yolks and beat until the mixture is smooth.

~ COOK'S TIP ~

The beaten egg whites give a light texture a bit like a soufflé.

5 ▲ In a large bowl, whisk the egg whites until they form stiff peaks. Fold them into the cornmeal mixture.

6 Pour into a well-greased 1.5 litre/ 2½ pint baking dish. Bake until puffed and brown, 30–40 minutes. Serve with a spoon from the baking dish, and pass butter on the side.

Charleston Cheese Corn Bread

SERVES 8

90g/3½oz/¾ cup yellow cornmeal

90g/3½oz/¾ cup plain (all-purpose) flour

10ml/2 tsp baking powder

5ml/1 tsp salt

3 eggs

175ml/6fl oz/¾ cup buttermilk

130g/4½oz/¾ cup chopped corn kernels
(fresh, frozen or canned)

75ml/2½fl oz/⅓ cup melted lard, white
cooking fat or vegetable oil

115g/4oz/1 cup grated mature (sharp)
Cheddar cheese

25g/1oz/2 tbsp butter or margarine

1 Preheat the oven to 200°C/400°F/
Gas 6.

~ VARIATION ~

For a spicier version, add one mild
chilli, seeded and finely chopped,
to the mixture.

2 ▲ In a large bowl, combine the
cornmeal, flour, baking powder and
salt. Stir to mix.

3 ▲ In a medium bowl, beat the eggs
until blended. Stir in the buttermilk,
corn, lard, white cooking fat or oil and
half the grated cheese.

4 Put the butter or margarine in a
20–23cm/ 8–9in frying pan (with
a heatproof handle) and place in the
oven. Heat until melted. Remove from
the oven and swirl the fat around to
coat the bottom and sides of the pan.

5 ▲ Add the liquid ingredients to the
dry ones and mix until just blended.
Pour the batter into the hot frying pan
and sprinkle with the remaining cheese.

6 Bake until the bread is golden brown
and shrinks slightly from the edges of
the frying pan, 25–30 minutes. Cut
into wedges and serve hot, with butter
or margarine.

Hush Puppies

SERVES 6

115g/4oz/1 cup plain (all-purpose) flour

10ml/2 tsp baking powder

5ml/1 tsp salt

115g/4oz/1 cup cornmeal, preferably
stoneground

40g/1½oz/½ cup finely chopped
spring onions (scallions)

1 egg, beaten

250ml/8fl oz/1 cup buttermilk

oil for deep-frying

1 Sift the flour, baking powder and
salt into a medium bowl. Stir in the
cornmeal and spring onions.

2 ▲ In a separate bowl, beat the egg
and buttermilk together. Stir rapidly
into the dry ingredients. Let the batter
rest for 20–30 minutes.

3 Heat oil in a deep-fryer or large,
heavy pan to 190°C/375°F (or when a
cube of bread browns in 40 seconds).

4 ▼ Drop the cornmeal mixture by
tablespoonfuls into the hot oil. If the
mixture seems too thick, add a little
more buttermilk. Fry until golden
brown. Drain on kitchen paper. Serve
the hush puppies hot.

Charleston Cheese Corn Bread (top), Hush Puppies

Cornmeal Scones

MAKES ABOUT 12

150g/5oz/1¼ cups plain (all-purpose) flour

12.5ml/2½ tsp baking powder

4ml/¾ tsp salt

50g/2oz/½ cup cornmeal, plus more for sprinkling

150g/5oz/⅓ cup cold butter, lard or white cooking fat, diced

175ml/6fl oz/¾ cup milk

1 Preheat the oven to 230°C/450°F/ Gas 8.

2 ▼ Sift the flour, baking powder and salt into a bowl. Stir in the cornmeal. Using your fingertips, rub the butter, lard or white cooking fat into the dry ingredients as quickly as possible until the mixture is crumbly and resembles breadcrumbs.

3 ▲ Make a well in the centre and pour in the milk. Stir in quickly with a wooden spoon until the dough begins to pull away from the sides of the bowl, about 1 minute.

4 ▲ Turn the dough onto a lightly floured surface and knead lightly 8–10 times only. Roll out to a thickness of 1cm/½in. Cut into rounds with a floured 5cm/2in pastry (cookie) cutter. Do not twist the cutter as you cut.

5 ▲ Sprinkle an ungreased baking sheet lightly with cornmeal. Arrange the scones on the sheet, about 2.5cm/1in apart. Sprinkle the tops of the scones with more cornmeal.

6 Bake until golden brown, about 10–12 minutes. Serve the scones hot, with butter or margarine.

French Quarter Beignets

MAKES ABOUT 20

225g/8oz/2 cups plain (all-purpose) flour

5ml/1 tsp salt

15ml/1 tbsp baking powder

5ml/1 tsp ground cinnamon

2 eggs

50g/2oz/¼ cup granulated sugar

175ml/6fl oz/¾ cup milk

2.5ml/½ tsp vanilla extract

oil for deep-frying

icing (confectioners') sugar, for sprinkling

1 ▲ To make the pastry, sift the flour, salt, baking powder and ground cinnamon into a medium mixing bowl.

2 ▲ In a separate bowl, beat together the eggs, granulated sugar, milk and vanilla. Pour the egg mixture into the dry ingredients and mix together quickly to form a ball.

3 Turn the pastry out on to a lightly floured surface and knead until it is smooth and elastic.

4 Heat the oil in a deep-fryer or large, heavy pan to 190°C/375°F.

5 ▼ Roll out the pastry to a round 5mm/¼in thick. Slice diagonally into diamonds about 7.5cm/3in long.

6 ▲ Fry in the hot oil, turning once, until golden brown on both sides. Remove with tongs or a slotted spoon and drain well on kitchen paper. Sprinkle the beignets with icing sugar before serving.

Georgia Peanut Butter Pie

SERVES 8

115g/4oz/2 cups fine digestive biscuit (graham cracker) crumbs

50g/2oz/¼ cup soft light brown sugar

75g/3oz/6 tbsp butter or margarine, melted

whipped cream or ice cream, to serve

FOR THE FILLING

3 egg yolks

90g/3½oz/½ cup granulated sugar

50g/2oz/¼ cup soft light brown sugar

25g/1oz/¼ cup cornflour (cornstarch)

pinch of salt

550ml/18fl oz/2½ cups evaporated milk

25g/1oz/2 tbsp butter or margarine

7.5ml/1½ tsp vanilla extract

115g/4oz/½ cup chunky peanut butter

90g/3½oz/¾ cup icing (confectioners') sugar

1 Preheat the oven to 180°C/350°F/ Gas 4.

2 ▲ Combine the biscuit crumbs, sugar and butter or margarine in a bowl and blend well. Spread the mixture in a well-greased 23cm/9in pie tin (pan), pressing evenly over the bottom and sides with your fingertips.

3 Bake the biscuit case for 10 minutes. Remove from the oven and leave to cool. Leave the oven on.

4 ▲ Combine the egg yolks, granulated and brown sugars, cornflour and salt in a heavy pan.

5 Slowly whisk in the milk. Cook over a medium heat, stirring constantly, until the mixture thickens, about 8–10 minutes. Reduce the heat to very low and cook until very thick, about 3–4 minutes more.

6 ▲ Beat in the butter or margarine. Stir in the vanilla. Remove from the heat. Cover the surface closely with clear film (plastic wrap) and cool.

~ VARIATIONS ~

If preferred, use an equal amount of finely crushed vanilla wafers or ginger nut biscuits (ginger snaps) in place of digestive biscuits for the base. Or make the pie with a ready-to-use digestive biscuit case.

7 ▲ In a small bowl combine the peanut butter with the icing sugar, working with your fingers to blend the ingredients to the consistency of small breadcrumbs.

8 ▲ Sprinkle all but 45ml/3 tbsp of the peanut butter crumbs evenly over the bottom of the biscuit case.

9 ▲ Pour in the filling, spreading it into an even layer. Sprinkle with the remaining crumbs. Bake for 15 minutes.

10 Leave the pie to cool for 1 hour. Serve with whipped cream or ice cream.

Mississippi Mud Cake

SERVES 8–10

225g/8oz/2 cups plain (all-purpose) flour

pinch of salt

5ml/1 tsp baking powder

300ml/½ pint/1¼ cups strong coffee

50ml/2fl oz/¼ cup whisky or brandy

150g/5oz plain (semisweet) chocolate

225g/8oz/1 cup butter or margarine

400g/14oz/2 cups granulated sugar

2 eggs, at room temperature

7.5ml/1½ tsp vanilla extract

unsweetened cocoa powder

sweetened whipped cream or ice cream,
   to serve (optional)

1 Preheat the oven to 140°C/275°F/
Gas 1.

2 Sift together the flour, salt and
baking powder.

3 ▼ Combine the coffee, whisky or
brandy, chocolate and butter or
margarine in the top of a double
boiler. Heat until the chocolate and
butter have melted and the mixture is
smooth, stirring occasionally.

4 ▲ Pour the chocolate mixture into
a large bowl. Using an electric mixer
on low speed, gradually beat in the
sugar. Continue beating until the
sugar has dissolved.

5 Raise the speed to medium and add
the sifted dry ingredients. Mix well,
then beat in the eggs and vanilla until
thoroughly blended.

6 Pour the mixture into a well-greased
3.5 litre/6 pint decorative ring mould
that has been dusted lightly with cocoa
powder. Bake until a skewer inserted in
the centre of the cake comes out clean,
about 1 hour 20 minutes.

7 ▲ Leave to cool in the pan for
15 minutes, then turn out on to a wire
rack. Leave to cool completely.

8 When the cake is cold, dust it
lightly with cocoa powder. Serve with
sweetened whipped cream or ice
cream, if you wish.

Banana Lemon Layer Cake

SERVES 8–10

250g/9oz/2¼ cups self-raising (self-rising) flour
6ml/1¼ tsp baking powder
2.5ml/½ tsp salt
115g/4oz/½ cup butter, softened
200g/7oz/1 cup granulated sugar
115g/4oz/½ cup soft light brown sugar
2 eggs
2.5ml/½ tsp grated lemon rind
3 very ripe bananas, mashed
5ml/1 tsp vanilla extract
50ml/2fl oz/¼ cup milk
75g/3oz/¾ cup chopped walnuts
FOR THE ICING
115g/4oz/½ cup butter, softened
500g/1¼lb/4½ cups icing (confectioners') sugar
4ml/¾ tsp grated lemon rind
45–75ml/3–5 tbsp fresh lemon juice

1 Preheat the oven to 180°C/350°F/Gas 4. Grease two 23cm/9in round cake tins (pans) and line the bottom of each with a disk of greased baking parchment.

2 Sift the flour with the baking powder and salt.

3 ▲ In a large mixing bowl, cream the butter with the sugars until light and fluffy. Beat in the eggs, one at a time. Stir in the lemon rind.

4 ▲ In a small bowl, mix the mashed bananas with the vanilla and milk. Add the banana mixture and the dry ingredients to the butter mixture alternately in two or three batches and stir until just blended. Fold in the nuts.

5 Divide the mixture between the cake tins and spread it out evenly. Bake until a skewer inserted in the centre comes out clean, 30–35 minutes. Leave to stand for 5 minutes before turning out on to a wire rack. Peel off the baking parchment and leave to cool.

6 For the icing, cream the butter until smooth, then gradually beat in the sugar. Stir in the lemon rind and enough juice to make a spreadable consistency.

7 ▼ Set one of the cake layers on a serving plate. Cover with about one-third of the icing. Top with the second cake layer. Spread the remaining icing evenly over the top and around the sides of the cake.

Southern Ambrosia

SERVES 6

4 large sweet oranges

1 fresh ripe pineapple

1 coconut

icing (confectioners') sugar (optional)

strips of fresh coconut or lime wedges,
  to garnish

1 Using a sharp knife, cut the peel
and pith off the oranges, working over
a bowl to catch the juices. Slice each
orange into very thin rounds and place
in the bowl with the juice.

2 ▲ Peel the pineapple. Cut into
quarters lengthways, and cut away the
core. Cut into thin slices.

3 Pierce the "eyes" of the coconut
with a screwdriver or ice pick. Drain
off the liquid. Using a heavy hammer,
crack the shell until it can be opened.
Prise out the white meat with a blunt
knife. Peel the dark brown skin from
the coconut meat and shred the meat
using the coarse blade of a grater or
food processor.

4 To assemble the dessert, layer the
fruits and coconut alternately in a
glass serving bowl. Sprinkle the layers
occasionally with a small amount of
icing sugar, if you like, to increase the
sweetness. Serve at once or chill before
eating. Garnish with strips of fresh
coconut or lime wedges before serving.

Pecan Pralines

MAKES ABOUT 30

350g/12oz/1½ cups soft light brown sugar

350g/12oz/1½ cups soft dark brown sugar

1.5ml/¼ tsp salt

120ml/4fl oz/½ cup milk

120ml/4fl oz/½ cup single (light) cream

25g/1oz/2 tbsp butter or margarine

5ml/1 tsp vanilla extract

175g/6oz/1 cup pecan pieces or halves

~ COOK'S TIP ~

To test for the soft ball stage
without a sugar thermometer,
drop a small amount of the
caramel into iced water. It should
form a ball that will hold its shape
and flatten readily when picked up
between the fingers.

1 ▲ In a heavy pan mix together the
sugars, salt, milk and cream. Stir
constantly until the mixture comes to
the boil. Cover the pan and cook,
without stirring, until crystals no
longer form on the sides of the pan,
about 3 minutes.

2 Uncover the pan and cook over a
medium heat, without stirring, to the
soft ball stage, 119°C/238°F on a sugar
thermometer.

3 Remove from the heat and beat in
the butter or margarine with a wooden
spoon. Continue beating until the
mixture is smooth and creamy and the
temperature of the mixture comes down
to 56°C/110°F. Beat in the vanilla and
the nuts.

4 ▼ Using two spoons, drop the pra-
line mixure by the spoonful on to a
baking sheet lined with buttered baking parchment. When cool, store the
pralines in an airtight container with
parchment between each of the layers.

Southern Ambrosia (top), Pecan Pralines

Pink Grapefruit Sorbet

<u>SERVES 8</u>

175g/6oz/¾ cup granulated sugar

120ml/4fl oz/½ cup water

1 litre/1¾ pints/4 cups strained freshly squeezed pink grapefruit juice

15–30ml/1–2 tbsp fresh lemon juice

icing (confectioners') sugar, to taste

1 In a small heavy pan, dissolve the granulated sugar in the water over a medium heat, without stirring. When the sugar has dissolved, boil for about 3–4 minutes. Remove from the heat and leave to cool.

2 ▼ Pour the cooled sugar syrup into the grapefruit juice. Stir well. Taste the mixture and adjust the flavour by adding some lemon juice or a little icing sugar, if necessary, but do not over-sweeten.

3 ▲ Pour the mixture into a metal or plastic freezer container and freeze until softly set, about 3 hours.

4 ▲ Remove from the container and chop roughly into 7.5cm/3in pieces. Place in a food processor and process until smooth. Return the mixture to the freezer container and freeze again until set. Repeat this freezing and chopping process two or three times, until a smooth consistency is obtained.

5 Alternatively, freeze the sorbet in an ice cream maker, following the manufacturer's instructions.

~ **VARIATION** ~

For Orange Sorbet, substitute an equal amount of orange juice for the grapefruit juice and increase the lemon juice to 45–60ml/ 3–4 tbsp, or to taste. For additional flavour, add 15ml/1 tbsp finely grated orange rind. If blood oranges are available, their deep red colour gives a dramatic effect, and the flavour is exciting as well.

Key Lime Sorbet

SERVES 4

250g/9oz/1¼ cups granulated sugar

550ml/18fl oz/2½ cups water

grated rind of 1 lime

175ml/6fl oz/¾ cup freshly squeezed
  lime juice

15–30ml/1–2 tbsp fresh lemon juice

icing (confectioners') sugar, to taste

1 ▲ In a small heavy pan, dissolve
the granulated sugar in the water,
without stirring, over a medium heat.
When the sugar has dissolved, boil for
5–6 minutes. Remove from the heat
and leave to cool.

2 ▲ Combine the cooled sugar syrup
and lime rind and juice in a measuring
jug (cup) or bowl. Stir well. Taste and
adjust the flavour by adding lemon
juice or some icing sugar, if necessary.
Do not over-sweeten.

3 ▲ Freeze the sorbet in an ice cream
maker, following the manufacturer's
instructions.

4 If you do not have an ice cream
maker, pour the mixture into a metal
or plastic freezer container and freeze
until softly set, about 3 hours.

5 Remove from the container and
chop roughly into 7.5cm/3in pieces.
Place in a food processor and process
until smooth. Return the mixture to
the freezer container and freeze again
until set. Repeat this freezing and
chopping process two or three times,
until a smooth consistency is obtained.

~ COOK'S TIP ~

If using an ice cream maker for
these sorbets, check the
manufacturer's instructions to
find out the freezing capacity.
If necessary, halve the
recipe quantities.

THE
MIDWEST

THE HEARTLAND OF AMERICA
CONTRIBUTES SIGNIFICANTLY TO
THE FOOD SUPPLY OF THE ENTIRE
COUNTRY, WITH GREAT FIELDS OF
WHEAT AND CORN, ORCHARDS AND
VERDANT FARMLAND. THE SYSTEM
OF WATERWAYS, INCLUDING THE
GREAT LAKES AND THE MISSISSIPPI,
HAS HISTORICALLY MOVED
PRODUCE TO OTHER REGIONS
WHILE PROVIDING A RICH SOURCE
OF FOOD AND BEAUTY.

Onion Soup with Mini Dumplings

SERVES 6

50g/2oz/¼ cup butter or margarine

30ml/2 tbsp olive oil

675g/1½lb onions, finely sliced

15ml/1 tbsp soft light brown sugar

5ml/1 tsp salt

2.5 litres/4 pints good beef stock or bouillon, homemade if possible

250ml/8fl oz/1 cup dry white wine

FOR THE MINI DUMPLINGS

1 egg

90g/3½oz/¾ cup–115g/4oz/1 cup plain (all-purpose) flour

2.5ml/½ tsp salt

pepper

1 Heat the butter or margarine with the oil in a large heavy pan. Add the onions and stir to coat well with the fats. Cover the pan and cook over a a low heat about 15 minutes, stirring occasionally.

2 ▲ Uncover the pan, add the sugar and salt, and continue cooking until the onions turn a rich brown colour. Stir often or the onions may burn.

3 ▲ Stir in the stock or bouillon and wine and bring to the boil. Lower the heat and simmer, partly covered, while you prepare the mini dumplings.

4 ▲ Beat the egg into a medium bowl. Add the flour, salt and pepper to taste and mix with a wooden spoon. Finish mixing with your fingers, rubbing to blend the egg and flour together. The pieces of dough should be pea-size or smaller.

5 ▲ Bring the soup back to the boil. Sprinkle in the pieces of dough, stirring gently. Reduce the heat and simmer for about 6 minutes, until the mini dumplings are slightly swollen and cooked through. Serve at once.

Split Pea Soup

SERVES 8

450g/1lb dried green split peas

2.5 litres/4 pints water

1 ham bone with some meat left on it, or 1 ham hock

2 onions, finely chopped

115g/4oz/1 cup sliced leeks

50g/2oz/½ cup finely sliced celery

15g/½oz/¼ cup fresh parsley sprigs

5ml/1 tsp salt

6 black peppercorns

2 bay leaves

1 ▲ Rinse the split peas under cold running water. Discard any discoloured peas. Place the peas in a large pan and add water to cover. Bring to the boil and boil for 2 minutes. Remove from the heat and leave to soak for 1 hour. Drain.

2 ▲ Put the peas back in the pan and add the measured water, ham bone or hock, onion, leeks, celery, parsley, salt, peppercorns and bay leaves. Bring to the boil. Reduce the heat, cover and simmer gently until the peas are tender, 1–1½ hours. Skim occasionally.

3 ▼ Remove the bay leaves and the ham bone or hock from the soup. Cut the meat off the bone, discarding any fat, and chop the meat finely. Set aside. Discard the ham bone and the bay leaves.

4 ▲ Purée the soup in batches in a food processor or blender. Pour into a clean pan and add the chopped ham. Check the seasoning. Simmer the soup for 3–4 minutes to heat right through before serving.

Spiced Pumpkin Soup

SERVES 6

45ml/3 tbsp olive oil

1 onion, sliced

6 spring onions (scallions), bulbs and
greens sliced separately

pinch of cayenne pepper

1.5ml/¼ tsp ground cumin

pinch of ground nutmeg or mace

1.2 litres/2 pints/5 cups chicken stock

800g/1¾lb/2½ cups pumpkin purée

2.5ml/½ tsp salt

250ml/8fl oz/1 cup single (light) cream

1 Heat the oil in a large heavy pan.
Add the onion and spring onion bulbs
and cook over a low heat until softened, 8–10 minutes.

2 ▲ Add the spices and stir well to
coat the onions. Cook for 3–4 minutes.
Add the pumpkin purée, stock and
salt. Raise the heat to medium; cook
for 15 minutes, stirring occasionally.

3 Let the soup cool slightly. Purée it
in a food processor or blender.

4 ▼ Return the soup to the pan.
Taste and add more cayenne, if
you like. Heat to simmering. Stir in
most of the cream and simmer
for 2–3 minutes more. Serve hot, with
a swirl of cream and some sliced
spring onion greens.

Indian Beef and Berry Soup

SERVES 4

30ml/2 tbsp vegetable oil

450g/1lb tender beef steak

3 onions, finely sliced

25g/1oz/2 tbsp butter

1 litre/1¾ pints/4 cups good beef stock
or bouillon

2.5ml/½ tsp salt

1 cup fresh huckleberries, blueberries or
blackberries, lightly mashed

15ml/1 tbsp honey

1 Heat the oil in a heavy pan until
almost smoking. Add the steak and
brown on both sides over medium-high
heat. Remove the steak and set aside.

2 Reduce the heat to low and add the
onions and butter to the pan. Stir well,
scraping up the meat juices. Cook
over a low heat until the onions are
softened, 8–10 minutes.

3 ▲ Add the stock or bouillon and
salt and bring to the boil, stirring well.
Mix in the berries and honey. Simmer
for 20 minutes.

4 Meanwhile, cut the steak into thin,
bitesize slivers.

5 ▼ Taste the soup and add more salt
or honey if necessary. Add the steak
and its juices to the pan. Stir, cook for
30 seconds and serve.

Spiced Pumpkin Soup (top), Indian Beef and Berry Soup

Dandelion Salad with Hot Bacon Dressing

SERVES 6

115g/4oz/about 2½ cups young tender
dandelion leaves or other sharp-flavoured
leaves such as rocket (arugula)

1 head of Boston, cos or romaine lettuce

4 spring onions (scallions), thinly sliced

8 bacon rashers (strips), cut across in
thin strips

50ml/2fl oz/¼ cup fresh lemon juice

30ml/2 tbsp granulated sugar

5ml/1 tsp Dijon-style mustard

pepper

1 Carefully pick over the dandelion
leaves and wash thoroughly in several
changes of water. Pat or spin dry.
Wash and dry the lettuce leaves.

2 ▼ Tear each lettuce and dandelion
leaf into two or three pieces. Arrange a
mixture of leaves on individual
serving plates. Sprinkle with the
sliced spring onions.

3 ▲ In a small frying pan, cook the
bacon until crisp. Remove the bacon
pieces with a slotted spoon and drain
on kitchen paper.

4 ▲ Add the lemon juice, sugar and
mustard to the bacon fat in the pan.
Heat the mixture gently for about
3–4 minutes, scraping up the browned
bits in the cooking juices and blending
in the mustard with a wooden spoon.

5 Spoon the hot dressing over the
salads and sprinkle with the bacon
pieces and freshly ground black
pepper. Serve at once.

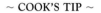

~ COOK'S TIP ~

Commercially grown dandelion
leaves are sometimes available
from specialist grocers. If picking
your own, choose leaves from
spring plants that have not yet
flowered, and use them fresh. After
flowering, the leaves of dandelions
become bitter and tough.

Vegetable Chilli

SERVES 8

50ml/2fl oz/¼ cup olive or vegetable oil

4 onions, chopped

50g/2oz/½ cup finely sliced celery

2–3 carrots, cut into 1cm/½ in cubes

2 garlic cloves, finely chopped

2.5ml/½ tsp celery seeds

1.5ml/¼ tsp cayenne pepper

5ml/1 tsp ground cumin

45ml/3 tbsp chilli powder

450g/1lb/2 cups canned chopped plum
   tomatoes with their juice

250ml/8fl oz/1 cup vegetable stock
   or water

7.5ml/1½ tsp salt

2.5ml/½ tsp fresh or dried thyme leaves

1 bay leaf

150g/5oz/2 cups cauliflower florets

250g/9oz/2 cups 1cm/½ in cubes of
   courgette (zucchini)

kernels from 1 corn on the cob

275g/10oz/2 cups cooked or canned
   kidney or pinto beans

hot pepper sauce (optional)

2 Stir in the celery seed, cayenne, cumin and chilli powder. Mix well. Add the tomatoes, stock or water, salt, thyme and bay leaf. Stir. Cook for 15 minutes, uncovered.

3 ▼ Add the cauliflower, courgette and corn. Cover and cook for a further 15 minutes.

4 ▲ Add the kidney or pinto beans, stir well and cook for 10 minutes more, uncovered. Check the seasoning, and add a dash of hot pepper sauce if you like. This is good with freshly boiled rice or baked potatoes.

1 ▲ Heat the oil in a large flameproof casserole or heavy pan and add the onions, celery, carrots and garlic. Cover the casserole and cook over a low heat, stirring from time to time, until the onions are softened, 8–10 minutes.

Stuffed Devilled Eggs

SERVES 6

6 hard-boiled eggs, peeled

40g/1½oz/¼ cup finely chopped cooked ham

6 walnut halves, finely chopped

15ml/1 tbsp finely chopped spring onion (scallion)

15ml/1 tbsp Dijon-style mustard

15ml/1 tbsp mayonnaise

10ml/2 tsp vinegar

1.5ml/¼ tsp salt

1.5ml/¼ tsp black pepper

1.5ml/¼ tsp cayenne pepper (optional)

paprika and a few slices of dill pickle, to garnish

1 Cut each egg in half lengthways. Place the yolks in a bowl and set the whites aside.

2 ▲ Mash the yolks well with a fork, or push them through a strainer. Add all the remaining ingredients and mix well with the yolks. Taste and adjust the seasoning if necessary.

3 ▼ Spoon the filling into the egg white halves, or pipe it in with a pastry bag and nozzle. Garnish the top of each stuffed egg with a little paprika and a small star or other shape cut from the pickle slices. Serve the stuffed eggs at room temperature.

Stuffed Celery Sticks

SERVES 4–6

12 crisp, tender celery sticks

25g/1oz/¼ cup crumbled blue cheese

115g/4oz/½ cup cream cheese

45ml/3 tbsp sour cream

50g/2oz/½ cup chopped walnuts

2 ▼ In a small bowl, combine the crumbled blue cheese, cream cheese and sour cream. Stir together with a wooden spoon until smoothly blended. Fold in all but 15ml/1 tbsp of the chopped walnuts.

3 ▲ Fill the celery pieces with the cheese mixture. Chill before serving, garnished with the reserved walnuts.

1 ▲ Trim the celery sticks and cut into 10cm/4in pieces.

~ **VARIATION** ~

Use the same filling to stuff scooped-out cherry tomatoes.

Stuffed Devilled Eggs, Stuffed Celery Sticks

Chicago Deep-pan Pizza

MAKES A 35CM/14IN PIZZA

1½ packets active dried yeast

250ml/8fl oz/1 cup lukewarm water

15ml/1 tbsp caster (superfine) sugar

440g/15½oz/3¾ cups plain
(all-purpose) flour

5ml/1 tsp salt

45ml/3 tbsp olive oil

FOR THE TOPPING

45ml/3 tbsp olive oil

275g/10oz/2½ cups diced
mozzarella cheese

500g/1¼lb/2½ cups peeled and chopped
tomatoes, preferably plum-type

40g/1½oz/½ cup freshly grated
Parmesan cheese

salt and pepper

25g/1oz/½ cup fresh basil leaves,
loosely packed

1 In a small bowl, mix the yeast with half the warm water. Stir in the sugar. Leave for 10 minutes.

2 Put the flour in a food processor with the steel blade. Add the salt. Pour in the yeast mixture, olive oil and the remaining warm water. Process until the dough begins to form a ball. If the dough is too sticky, add a little more flour. If it will not mass together, add a little more warm water and process again.

3 Turn the dough on to a lightly floured surface. Knead until smooth, about 5 minutes. Form into a ball and place in a lightly oiled large bowl. Cover with a damp dish towel. Leave to rise in a warm place until the dough doubles its volume, about 1½ hours.

4 Preheat the oven to 240°C/475°F/ Gas 9.

5 ▲ Knock back (punch down) the dough and knead it lightly for about 2–3 minutes. Set it in the centre of an oiled 35cm/14in diameter pizza pan. Using your fingertips, stretch and pat out the dough to line the pan evenly.

6 ▲ Prick the dough evenly all over with a fork. Bake for 5 minutes.

7 ▲ Brush the pizza dough base with 15ml/1 tbsp of the olive oil. Sprinkle with the mozzarella, leaving the rim clear. Spoon the tomatoes over the mozzarella and sprinkle with the Parmesan. Season and drizzle over the remaining olive oil.

8 Bake until the crust is golden brown and the topping is bubbling hot, 25–30 minutes. Scatter over the basil leaves and serve.

Pirozhki with Ham Filling

MAKES 12

25g/1oz/2 tbsp butter or margarine

½ onion, finely chopped

175g/6oz/1½ cups finely chopped ham

120ml/4fl oz/½ cup whipping cream

30ml/2 tbsp finely chopped fresh parsley

15ml/1 tbsp Worcestershire sauce

salt and pepper

FOR THE PASTRY

225g/8oz/2 cups plain (all-purpose) flour

5ml/1 tsp salt

12.5ml/2½ tsp baking powder

115g/4oz/½ cup cold butter, lard or white
  cooking fat, diced

45–60ml/3–4 tbsp milk, plus more
  for brushing

1 ▲ Melt the butter or margarine in
a small frying pan. Add the onions and
cook over a low heat until soft and
golden, 10–12 minutes. Add the ham
and cook for 2–3 minutes more, stirring.

2 ▲ Turn the onion and ham
mixture into a bowl. Leave to cool
slightly, then stir in the cream, parsley
and Worcestershire sauce. Season with
salt and pepper.

3 Preheat oven to 230°C/450°F/Gas 8.

4 ▲ For the pastry, sift the flour,
salt and baking powder into a bowl.
With a pastry blender, cut in the
butter, lard or white cooking fat until
the mixture resembles breadcrumbs,
or rub in with your fingertips.

5 Make a well in the centre and add
the milk. Stir with a fork until the
mixture begins to pull away from the
sides of the bowl, no more than
1 minute. (If overmixed, the pastry
will not be as light and tender.)

6 Turn the pastry on to a lightly
floured surface and knead lightly for
less than 1 minute. Roll out to 6mm/
¼in thick. Cut into 7.5cm/3in squares.

7 ▲ Place a spoonful of the ham
filling in the centre of each pastry
square. Brush the edges with milk and
fold the pastry over to form a
triangular shape. Press the edges
together with a fork to seal.

8 Arrange the triangles on a baking
sheet and brush them with milk. Bake
until the pastry is golden and cooked,
about 30 minutes.

Pan-fried Honey Chicken Drumsticks

SERVES 4

120ml/4fl oz/½ cup honey

juice of 1 lemon

30ml/2 tbsp soy sauce

15ml/1 tbsp sesame seeds

2.5ml/½ tsp fresh or dried thyme leaves

12 chicken drumsticks

2.5ml/½ tsp salt

2.5ml/½ tsp pepper

90g/3½oz/¾ cup plain (all-purpose) flour

45ml/3 tbsp butter or margarine

45ml/3 tbsp vegetable oil

120ml/4fl oz/½ cup white wine

120ml/4fl oz/½ cup chicken stock

1 In a large bowl, combine the honey, lemon juice, soy sauce, sesame seeds and thyme. Add the drumsticks and mix to coat them well. Leave to marinate in a cool place for 2 hours or more, turning occasionally.

2 ▲ Mix the salt, pepper and flour in a shallow bowl. Drain the drumsticks, reserving the marinade. Roll them in the seasoned flour to coat all over.

3 Heat the butter or margarine with the oil in a large heavy frying pan. When hot and sizzling, add the drumsticks. Brown on all sides. Reduce the heat to medium-low and cook until the chicken is done, 12–15 minutes.

4 Test with a fork to see if the chicken is done; the juices should be clear. Remove the drumsticks to a serving dish and keep hot.

5 ▲ Pour off most of the fat from the pan. Add the wine, stock and reserved marinade and stir well to mix in the cooking juices on the bottom of the pan. Bring to the boil and simmer until reduced by half. Check for seasoning, then spoon this sauce over the drumsticks and serve.

Oatmeal Pan-fried Trout

SERVES 4

135g/4¾oz/1½ cups rolled oats

salt and pepper

4 medium river trout, cleaned,
  heads and tails left on if desired

75g/3oz/6 tbsp butter or margarine

lemon halves, to serve

1 Grind the oats in a food processor or blender until they are the texture of fine meal. Turn into a shallow dish and spread out evenly. Season with salt and pepper.

2 Rinse the trout and dry well with kitchen paper.

3 Melt the butter or margarine in a large frying pan over a low heat.

4 ▲ Dip both sides of each trout in the butter or margarine, then roll in the ground oats, patting with your fingers to help the oats stick.

5 ▼ Put the fish in the frying pan in one layer. Increase the heat to medium and cook until golden brown, about 3–4 minutes on each side. (Cook in batches, if necessary, using more butter or margarine.) Serve hot, with lemon halves on the side.

Pan-fried Honey Chicken Drumsticks (top), Oatmeal Pan-fried Trout

Savoury Sausage Scones

SERVES 4

200g/7oz/1¾ cups plain (all-purpose) flour

5ml/1 tsp salt

12.5ml/2½ tsp baking powder

50g/2oz/¼ cup cold butter, lard or
    white cooking fat, diced

175ml/6fl oz/¾ cup plus 45ml/3 tbsp milk

FOR THE GRAVY

40g/1½oz/3 tbsp butter or margarine

45ml/3 tbsp finely chopped onion

350g/12oz lean pork sausage meat
    (bulk sausage)

25g/1oz/¼ cup plain (all-purpose) flour

475ml/16fl oz/2 cups milk, warmed

1.5ml/¼ tsp paprika

15ml/1 tbsp chopped fresh parsley

1 Preheat oven to 230°C/450°F/Gas 8.

2 For the savoury scones, sift the flour, salt and baking powder into a mixing bowl. Using your fingertips, rub the butter, lard or white cooking fat into the dry ingredients until the mixture is crumbly and resembles breadcrumbs.

3 Make a well in the centre and add the 175ml/6fl oz/¾ cup milk. Stir with a wooden spoon until the dough begins to come away from the sides of the bowl, less than 1 minute. (Do not overmix the dough or the scones will not be light and tender.)

4 Turn the dough on to a lightly floured surface and knead gently for about ½ minute, making 8–10 folds only. Roll out to about 2cm/¾in thick. Cut out rounds using a 6cm/2½in pastry (cookie) cutter. Do not twist the cutter.

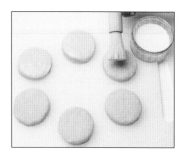

5 ▲ Brush the tops of the rounds with the 45ml/3 tbsp of milk. Arrange on a lightly greased baking sheet. Bake until puffed and lightly golden, 12–15 minutes.

6 While the scones are baking, make the sausage sauce. Melt the butter or margarine in a heavy pan. Add the onion and cook for 3–4 minutes. Add the sausage meat and cook over a medium-low heat until lightly browned and crumbly. Do not overcook. Drain off the excess fat in the pan, leaving about 30–45ml/2–3 tbsp.

7 ▲ Sprinkle the flour over the sausage mixture in the pan. Stir well to blend thoroughly.

8 Slowly add the warmed milk, blending it in well and scraping up the pan juices. Simmer until thickened. Add the paprika and parsley.

9 Split the scones and place on individual serving plates. Spoon the sauce on top and serve at once.

Twin Cities Meatballs

Serves 6

25g/1oz/2 tbsp butter or margarine

½ onion, finely chopped

350g/12oz rump (round) steak mince

115g/4oz veal mince

225g/8oz lean pork mince

1 egg

40g/1½oz/½ cup mashed potatoes

30ml/2 tbsp finely chopped fresh dill
  or parsley

1 garlic clove, finely chopped

5ml/1 tsp salt

2.5ml/½ tsp pepper

2.5ml/½ tsp ground allspice

1.5ml/¼ tsp ground nutmeg

40g/1½oz/¾ cup fresh breadcrumbs

175ml/6fl oz/¾ cup milk

25g/1oz/¼ cup plus 15ml/1 tbsp plain
  (all-purpose) flour

30ml/2 tbsp olive oil

175ml/6fl oz/¾ cup pouring (half-and-
  half) cream or evaporated milk

buttered noodles, to serve

1 Melt the butter or margarine in a large frying pan. Add the onion and cook over a low heat until softened, 8–10 minutes. Remove from the heat. Using a slotted spoon, transfer the onion to a large mixing bowl.

2 ▲ Add the minced meats, egg, mashed potatoes, dill or parsley, garlic, salt, pepper, allspice and nutmeg to the bowl.

3 Put the breadcrumbs in a small bowl and add the milk. Stir until well moistened, then add to the other ingredients. Mix well.

4 ▲ Shape the mixture into balls about 2.5cm/1in in diameter. Roll them in 25g/1oz/¼ cup of the flour to coat all over.

5 Add the olive oil to the pan and heat over a a medium heat. Add the meatballs and brown on all sides, 8–10 minutes. Shake the pan occasionally to roll the balls so that they colour evenly. With a slotted spoon, remove the meatballs to a serving dish. Cover with foil and keep warm.

6 ▲ Stir the 15ml/1 tbsp of flour into the fat in the pan. Add the pouring cream or evaporated milk and mix in with a small whisk. Simmer for 3–4 minutes. Check the seasoning.

7 Pour the sauce over the meatballs. Serve hot with noodles.

~ COOK'S TIP ~

The meatballs are also good for a buffet or cocktail party. To serve with drinks, omit the sauce.

Country Meat Loaf

SERVES 6

25g/1oz/2 tbsp butter or margarine
1 onion, finely chopped
2 garlic cloves, finely chopped
50g/2oz/½ cup finely chopped celery
450g/1lb lean ground beef
225g/8oz veal mince
225g/8oz lean pork mince
2 eggs
50g/2oz/1 cup fine fresh breadcrumbs
25g/1oz/½ cup chopped fresh parsley
30ml/2 tbsp chopped fresh basil
2.5ml/½ tsp fresh or dried thyme leaves
2.5ml/½ tsp salt
2.5ml/½ tsp pepper
30ml/2 tbsp Worcestershire sauce
50ml/2fl oz/¼ cup chilli sauce or tomato ketchup
6 bacon rashers (strips)

1 Preheat oven to 180°C/350°F/Gas 4.

2 ▼ Melt the butter or margarine in a small frying pan over a low heat. Add the onion, garlic and celery and cook until softened, 8–10 minutes. Remove from the heat and leave to cool slightly.

3 ▲ In a large mixing bowl, combine the onion, garlic and celery with all the other ingredients except the bacon. Mix together lightly, using a fork or your fingers. Do not overwork or the meat loaf will be too compact.

4 ▲ Form the meat mixture into an oval loaf. Carefully transfer it to a shallow baking tin (pan).

5 ▲ Lay the bacon slices across the meat loaf. Bake for 1¼ hours, basting occasionally with the juices and bacon fat in the pan.

6 Remove from the oven and drain off the fat. Leave the meat loaf to stand for 10 minutes before serving.

Spareribs with Sauerkraut

SERVES 4

1.3–1.8kg/3–4lb spareribs, cut in individual portions

½ onion, finely chopped

50ml/2fl oz/¼ cup Worcestershire sauce

15ml/1 tbsp dry mustard

2.5ml/½ tsp paprika

5ml/1 tsp salt

750ml/1¼ pints/3 cups flat beer

45ml/3 tbsp olive or vegetable oil

1.75 litres/3 pints sauerkraut, canned or bulk

1 tart-sweet apple, peeled, cored and sliced

5ml/1 tsp caraway seeds

parsley, for garnishing

1 Arrange the ribs in a single layer in a large baking dish.

2 ▲ In a large measuring jug (cup), combine the onion, Worcestershire sauce, mustard, paprika, salt and beer. Mix well. Pour the mixture evenly over the ribs. Leave to marinate for at least 2 hours, basting occasionally.

3 Preheat the oven to 190°C/375°F/ Gas 5.

4 Remove the ribs from the dish and pat dry with kitchen paper. Reserve the marinade.

5 ▲ Heat the oil in a flameproof casserole. Brown the ribs, turning to sear them on all sides. Work in batches, if necessary. Pour in the marinade. Transfer the casserole to the oven. Bake for 35–40 minutes, turning the ribs occasionally.

6 Rinse the sauerkraut, if desired, and drain well. Mix with the apple and caraway seeds.

7 ▼ Remove the casserole from the oven. Holding the ribs to one side, distribute the sauerkraut mixture evenly in the bottom of the casserole. Arrange the ribs on top of the kraut, pushing them down evenly.

8 Return to the oven and bake until the meat on the ribs is tender, about 45–60 minutes more. Serve the ribs on a large heated platter, on a bed of sauerkraut, garnished with parsley.

Baked Pork Loin with Red Cabbage and Apples

SERVES 8

2kg/4½lb boned loin of pork

2.5ml/½ tsp ground ginger

salt and pepper

60ml/4 tbsp melted butter

about 350ml/12fl oz/1½ cups sweet apple cider or dry white wine

FOR THE CABBAGE

40g/1½oz/3 tbsp butter or margarine

3 onions, finely sliced

5ml/1 tsp caraway seeds

3 tart-sweet apples, quartered, cored and sliced

15ml/1 tbsp soft dark brown sugar

1.6kg/3½lb head of red cabbage, cored and shredded

90ml/6 tbsp cider vinegar, or 50ml/2fl oz/¼ cup wine vinegar and 30ml/2 tbsp water

120ml/4fl oz/½ cup beef stock

120ml/4fl oz/½ cup sweet apple cider or white wine

5ml/1 tsp salt

1.5ml/¼ tsp fresh or dried thyme leaves

1 Preheat oven to 180°F/350°F/Gas 4.

2 ▲ Trim any excess fat from the pork roast. Tie it into a neat shape, if necessary. Sprinkle with the ginger, salt and pepper.

3 ▲ Place the pork, fat side down, in a large casserole. Cook over a medium heat, turning frequently, until browned on all sides, about 15 minutes. Add a little of the melted butter if the roast starts to stick.

4 Cover, transfer to the oven and roast for 1 hour, basting frequently with the pan drippings, melted butter and cider or wine.

5 ▲ Meanwhile, to prepare the cabbage, melt the butter or margarine in a large frying pan and add the onions and caraway seeds. Cook over a low heat until softened, 8–10 minutes. Stir in the apple slices and brown sugar. Cover the pan and cook for 4–5 minutes more.

6 Stir in the cabbage. Add the vinegar. Cover and cook for 10 minutes. Pour in the stock and cider or wine, add the salt and thyme leaves, and stir well. Cover again and cook over a medium-low heat for 30 minutes.

7 ▲ After this time, remove the pot from the oven. Transfer the roast to a plate and keep hot. Tilt the casserole and spoon off and discard all but 30ml/2 tbsp of the fat.

8 ▲ Transfer the cabbage mixture from the frying pan to the casserole and stir well to mix thoroughly with the roasting juices.

9 ▲ Place the pork roast on top of the layer of cabbage. Cover and return to the oven. Cook for another hour, basting occasionally with cider or wine.

Spicy Sauerbraten with Ginger Nut Gravy

SERVES 8

1.8kg/4lb beef chuck roast or boneless
venison shoulder roast

10ml/2 tsp salt

pepper

2 onions, sliced

100g/3½oz/½ cup sliced carrots

2 bay leaves

5ml/1 tsp black peppercorns

12 juniper berries

6 whole cloves

5ml/1 tsp dry mustard

a few blades of mace

475ml/2 cups wine vinegar

475ml/2 cups boiling water

50ml/2fl oz/¼ cup vegetable oil or butter

15ml/1 tbsp soft dark brown sugar

65g/2½oz/¾ cup crushed ginger nut
biscuits (gingersnaps)

noodles, to serve (optional)

1 ▲ Rub the roast with the salt and
some freshly ground black pepper.

~ COOK'S TIP ~

In braising, meat is browned or
seared in hot fat on all sides to seal
in the juices before being cooked
slowly in liquid. Check the
sauerbraten after about 30 minutes
of baking to make sure that the
cooking liquid is simmering slowly,
not boiling. If necessary, lower
the oven temperature slightly.

2 ▲ In a deep earthenware or non-
metallic bowl, combine the onions,
carrots, bay leaves, peppercorns,
juniper berries, cloves, mustard, mace
and vinegar. Mix well. Stir in the
boiling water.

3 ▲ Set the meat in the bowl and add
more water if necessary: the meat should
be at least half covered. Cover tightly
and chill for at least 48 hours and up
to 4 days. Turn the meat once a day.

4 Preheat the oven to 180°C/350°F/
Gas 4.

5 ▲ Remove the meat, reserving the
marinade. Pat it dry with kitchen paper.
Heat the oil or butter in a large
flameproof casserole and brown the
meat on all sides. This will take about
15 minutes.

6 ▲ Add the onions and carrots from
the marinade, as well as 475ml/16fl oz/
2 cups of the liquid. Reserve the remaining marinade. Cover the casserole and
transfer to the oven. Cook for 4 hours.

7 ▲ Remove the meat to a hot
serving dish. Press the vegetables and
liquids from the casserole through a
fine strainer. There should be about
600ml/1 pint/2½ cups strained liquid;
if necessary, add a little more of the
marinade liquid. Pour into a pan.

8 ▲ Boil until slightly reduced and
thickened, about 5 minutes. Stir in the
brown sugar and ginger nut crumbs.
Adjust the seasoning if necessary.

9 Slice the meat. Serve with the hot
ginger nut gravy and boiled noodles,
if you like.

Mashed Carrots and Parsnips

SERVES 6

450g/1lb parsnips, cut into 1cm/½in slices

450g/1lb carrots, cut into 1cm/½in slices

1 onion, chopped

1 bay leaf

10ml/2 tsp granulated sugar

1.5ml/¼ tsp salt

250ml/8fl oz/1 cup water

30ml/2 tbsp butter or olive oil

finely chopped fresh chives, to garnish

1 Put the parsnip and carrot slices in a medium pan with the chopped onion, bay leaf, sugar and salt. Add the water.

2 ▼ Cover the pan tightly and cook over a medium heat, stirring occasionally, until the vegetables are just tender, about 20 minutes. Check from time to time to make sure the water has not evaporated, adding a little more if necessary.

3 ▲ Drain most of the water from the vegetables and discard the bay leaf. Purée the vegetables in a food processor or food mill. Beat in the butter or oil and turn into a warmed serving dish. Sprinkle with the chives and serve at once.

Baked Acorn Squash with Herbs

SERVES 4

2 acorn squash

90ml/6 tbsp mixed finely chopped fresh chives, thyme, basil and parsley

50g/2oz/¼ cup butter or margarine

salt and pepper

1 ▲ Cut each squash in half crossways and scoop out the seeds and stringy fibres. If necessary, cut a small slice off the base of each squash half so that it sits level.

2 Preheat oven to 190°C/375°F/Gas 5.

3 ▼ Divide the herbs in four, and spoon into the squash half hollows.

~ VARIATION ~

For Caramel-baked Acorn Squash, replace the herbs with 45ml/3 tbsp soft dark brown sugar. Melt the butter or margarine, dissolve the brown sugar in it and fill squashes.

4 ▲ Top each half with 15ml/1 tbsp butter or margarine and season with salt and pepper.

5 Arrange the squash halves in a shallow baking dish large enough to hold them in one layer. Pour boiling water into the bottom of the dish, to a depth of about 2.5cm/1in. Cover the squash loosely with a piece of foil.

6 Bake until the squash is tender when tested with a fork, ¾–1 hour. Serve hot, keeping the halves upright.

Mashed Carrots and Parsnips (top), Baked Acorn Squash with Herbs

Wisconsin Cheddar and Chive Biscuits

MAKES ABOUT 20

200g/7oz/1¾ cups plain (all-purpose) flour

10ml/2 tsp baking powder

2.5ml/½ tsp bicarbonate of soda (baking soda)

1.5ml/¼ tsp salt

1.5ml/¼ tsp pepper

65g/2½oz/5 tbsp cold unsalted butter, diced

50g/2oz/½ cup grated mature (sharp) Cheddar cheese

30ml/2 tbsp finely chopped fresh chives

175ml/6fl oz/¾ cup buttermilk

~ **VARIATION** ~

For Cheddar and Bacon Biscuits, substitute 45ml/3 tbsp crumbled cooked bacon for the chives.

1 Preheat oven to 200°C/400°F/Gas 6.

2 ▲ Sift the flour, baking powder, bicarbonate of soda, salt and pepper into a large bowl. Using your fingertips, rub the butter into the dry ingredients until the mixture is crumbly and resembles breadcrumbs. Add the cheese and chives and stir to blend.

3 Make a well in the centre of the mixture. Add the buttermilk and stir vigorously until the mixture comes away from the sides of the bowl, 1 minute.

4 ▼ Drop 30ml/2 tbsp mounds spaced 5–7.5cm/2–3in apart on a lightly greased baking sheet. Bake until golden brown, 12–15 minutes.

Corn Oysters

MAKES ABOUT 8

150g/5oz/1 cup grated fresh corn

1 egg, separated

30ml/2 tbsp plain (all-purpose) flour

1.5ml/¼ tsp salt

1.5ml/¼ tsp pepper

30–60ml/2–4 tbsp butter or margarine

30–60ml/2–4 tbsp vegetable oil

1 Combine the corn, egg yolk and flour in a bowl. Mix well. Add the salt and pepper.

~ **COOK'S TIP** ~

Thawed frozen or canned corn kernels can also be used. Drain them well and chop.

2 ▲ In a separate bowl, whisk the egg white until it forms stiff peaks. Fold it carefully into the corn mixture.

3 Heat 30ml/2 tbsp of the butter or margarine with 30ml/2 tbsp of the oil in a frying pan. When the fats are very hot and almost smoking, drop tablespoonfuls of the corn mixture into the pan. Fry until crisp and brown on the bases.

4 ▼ Turn the "oysters" over and cook for 1–2 minutes on the other side. Drain on kitchen paper and keep hot. Continue frying the "oysters", adding more fat as necessary.

5 Serve hot as an accompaniment to meat or chicken dishes, or by themselves as a light dish with a mixed salad.

Wisconsin Cheddar and Chive Biscuits (top), Corn Oysters

Milwaukee Onion Tart

SERVES 6

30ml/2 tbsp butter or olive oil
5 onions, thinly sliced
2.5ml/½ tsp salt
2.5ml/½ tsp fresh or dried thyme leaves
1.5ml/¼ tsp pepper
1 egg
120ml/4fl oz/½ cup sour cream or natural (plain) yogurt
10ml/2 tsp poppy seeds
1.5ml/¼ tsp ground mace or nutmeg

FOR THE PASTRY

115g/4oz/1 cup plain (all-purpose) flour
6ml/1¼ tsp baking powder
2.5ml/½ tsp salt
40g/1½oz/3 tbsp cold butter, lard or white cooking fat, diced
30–45ml/2–3 tbsp milk

1 ▲ Heat the butter or oil in a medium frying pan. Add the onions and cook over a low heat until soft and golden, 10–12 minutes. Season with the salt, thyme and pepper. Remove from the heat and leave to cool.

2 Preheat the oven to 220°C/425°F/ Gas 7.

3 ▲ For the pastry, sift the flour, baking powder and salt into a bowl. Using your fingertips, rub the butter, lard or white cooking fat into the dry ingredients until the mixture is crumbly and resembles breadcrumbs. Add the milk and stir in lightly with a wooden spoon to make a dough.

4 Turn the pastry out on to a floured surface and knead lightly for 30 seconds.

5 Pat out the pastry into a disc about 20cm/8in in diameter. Transfer to a 20cm/8in baking tin (pan) that is at least 5cm/2in deep. Press the pastry into an even layer. Cover with the onions.

6 ▲ Beat together the egg and sour cream or yogurt. Spread evenly over the onions. Sprinkle with the poppy seeds and mace or nutmeg. Bake until the egg topping is puffed and golden, 25–30 minutes.

7 Leave to cool in the pan for 10 minutes. Slip a knife between the tart and the tin to loosen, then turn out on to a plate. Cut the onion tart into wedges and serve warm.

Huckleberry Cake

SERVES 10

225g/8oz/2 cups plain (all-purpose) flour

15ml/1 tbsp baking powder

5ml/1 tsp salt

65g/2½oz/⅓ cup butter or margarine, at room temperature

150g/5oz/¾ cup granulated sugar

1 egg

250ml/8fl oz/1 cup milk

2.5ml/½ tsp grated lemon rind

225g/8oz/2 cups fresh or frozen huckleberries, well drained

115g/4oz/1 cup icing (confectioners') sugar

30ml/2 tbsp fresh lemon juice

1 Preheat the oven to 180°C/350°F/ Gas 4.

2 ▲ Sift the flour with the baking powder and salt.

3 ▲ In a large bowl, beat the butter or margarine with the granulated sugar until light and fluffy. Beat in the egg and milk. Fold in the flour mixture, mixing well until evenly blended. Mix in the lemon rind.

4 ▼ Spread half the mixture in a greased 15 × 3½ × 5cm/13 × 9 × 2in baking dish. Sprinkle with 250ml/8fl oz/ 1 cup of the berries. Top with the remaining mixture and sprinkle with the rest of the berries. Bake until golden brown and a skewer inserted in the centre comes out clean, 35–45 minutes.

5 ▲ Mix the icing sugar gradually into the lemon juice to make a smooth glaze with a pourable consistency. Drizzle the glaze over the top of the cake and allow it to set before serving, still warm or at room temperature.

Pickled Eggs and Beetroot

SERVES 8

900g/2lb small beetroot, cooked and peeled

350ml/12fl oz/1½ cups cider vinegar

350ml/12fl oz/1½ cups beetroot cooking liquid or water

90g/3½oz/½ cup granulated sugar

1 bay leaf

5ml/1 tsp salt

15ml/1 tbsp whole allspice berries

5ml/1 tsp whole cloves

2.5ml/½ tsp ground ginger

2.5ml/½ tsp caraway seeds

8 hard-boiled eggs, shelled

1 ▲ Place the beetroot in a very large glass jar, or in several smaller jars.

2 Combine the vinegar, beetroot liquid or water, sugar, bay leaf, salt and spices in a pan. Heat, stirring to dissolve the sugar. Simmer for 5 minutes.

3 Pour the mixture over the beetroot. Leave to cool completely.

4 ▼ Add the eggs to the jar(s) of beetroot. Cover and chill for 2–3 days before serving. The pickle will keep for up to a week in the refrigerator.

Pickled Cucumber and Onion

MAKES ABOUT 1 LITRE/1¾ PINTS/4 CUPS

900g/2lb cucumbers, scrubbed and cut into 6mm/¼in slices

4 onions, very thinly sliced

30ml/2 tbsp salt

350ml/12fl oz/1½ cups cider vinegar

300g/11oz/1½ cups granulated sugar

30ml/2 tbsp mustard seeds

30ml/2 tbsp celery seeds

1.5ml/¼ tsp turmeric

1.5ml/¼ tsp cayenne pepper

1 ▲ Put the sliced cucumbers and onions in a large bowl and sprinkle with the salt. Mix well. Cover loosely and leave to stand for 3 hours.

2 Drain the vegetables. Rinse well under cold water and drain again.

3 Prepare some heatproof glass jars (such as bottling jars). Wash them well in warm soapy water and rinse thoroughly in warm water. Put them in a 150°C/300°F/Gas 2 oven and heat for 30 minutes to sterilize them. Keep the jars hot until ready to use.

4 ▼ Combine the remaining ingredients in a large non-metallic pan and bring to the boil. Add the cucumbers and onions. Reduce the heat and simmer for 2–3 minutes. Do not boil or the pickles will be limp.

5 ▲ Spoon the hot vegetables into the hot jars. Add enough of the hot liquid to come to 1cm/½in from the top. Carefully wipe the jar rims with a clean damp cloth.

6 To seal, cover the surface of the pickles with a waxed disc, wax side down, then put on the jar lid. The pickles should be sealed immediately. If the lid does not have a rubber seal, first cover the top of the jar with clear film (plastic wrap) or cellophane and then screw a plastic top down over it. Avoid using metal, as it may rust. Store in a cool dark place for at least 4 weeks before serving.

Pickled Eggs and Beetroot (centre), Pickled Cucumber and Onion

Rhubarb Pie

SERVES 6

175g/6oz/1½ cups plain (all-purpose) flour

2.5ml/½ tsp salt

10ml/2 tsp granulated sugar

75g/3oz/6 tbsp cold butter, lard or
  white cooking fat, diced

30–45ml/2–3 tbsp iced water

30ml/2 tbsp whipping cream

FOR THE FILLING

900g/2lb fresh rhubarb, cut into
  1–2.5cm/½–1in slices

30ml/2 tbsp cornflour (cornstarch)

1 egg

300g/11oz/1½ cups granulated sugar

15ml/1 tbsp grated orange rind

1 ▲ For the pastry, sift the flour, salt
and sugar into a bowl. With a pastry
blender, cut in the butter, lard or
white cooking fat until the mixture
resembles breadcrumbs, or rub in
with your fingertips.

2 Sprinkle with 30ml/2 tbsp of the iced
water and mix until the pastry holds
together. If the pastry is too crumbly, add
a little more water, 5ml/1 tsp at a time.

~ COOK'S TIP ~

Be sure to cut off and discard the
green rhubarb leaves from the
pink stalks, as they are toxic
and not edible.

3 ▲ Gather the pastry into a ball,
flatten into a disk, wrap in clear film
(plastic wrap) and chill for 20 minutes.

4 ▲ Roll out the pastry between two
sheets of clear film to a thickness of
about 3mm/⅛in. Use to line a 23cm/
9in pie tin (pan). Trim all around,
leaving a 1cm/½in overhang. Fold the
overhang under the edge and flute.
Chill the pastry case (pie shell) and
trimmings for 30 minutes.

5 ▲ For the filling, put the rhubarb
in a bowl and sprinkle with the
cornflour. Toss to coat.

6 Preheat oven to 220°C/425°F/Gas 7.

7 In a small bowl, beat the egg with
the sugar. Mix in the orange rind.

8 ▲ Stir the sugar mixture into the
rhubarb and mix well. Spoon the fruit
into the pastry case.

9 ▲ Roll out the pastry trimmings.
Stamp out decorative shapes with a
pastry (cookie) cutter or cut shapes
with a small knife, using a cardboard
template as a guide, if you like.

10 Arrange the shapes on top of the
pie. Brush the trimmings and the edge
of the pastry case with cream.

11 Bake for 30 minutes. Reduce the
heat to 160°C/325°F/Gas 3 and
continue baking until the pastry is
golden brown and the rhubarb is tender,
about 15–20 minutes more.

Brown Sugar Tart

SERVES 8

175g/6oz/1½ cups plain (all-purpose) flour

2.5ml/½ tsp salt

10ml/2 tsp granulated sugar

75g/3oz/6 tbsp cold butter or lard, diced

30–45ml/2–3 tbsp iced water

FOR THE FILLING

25g/1oz/¼ cup plain (all-purpose)
flour, sifted

225g/8oz/1 cup soft light brown sugar

2.5ml/½ tsp vanilla extract

350ml/12fl oz/1½ cups whipping cream

40g/1½oz/3 tbsp butter, finely diced

pinch of grated nutmeg

1 Sift the flour, salt and sugar into a
bowl. Using your fingertips, rub the
butter or lard into the dry ingredients
until the mixture resembles breadcrumbs.

2 ▲ Sprinkle with 30ml/2 tbsp of the
water and mix until the pastry holds
together. If it is too crumbly, add more
water, 5ml/1 tsp at a time. Gather into
a ball and flatten. Wrap in clear film
(plastic wrap) and chill for 20 minutes.

3 Roll out the pastry to about 3mm/
⅛in thick and line a 23cm/9in tart tin
(pan). Trim all around, leaving a 1cm/
½in overhang. Fold it under and flute
the edge. Chill for 30 minutes.

4 Preheat oven to 220°C/425°F/Gas 7.

5 Line the pastry case (pie shell)with
a piece of baking parchment 5cm/2in
larger all around than the diameter of
the tin. Fill the case with dried beans.
Bake until the pastry has just set, 8–10
minutes. Remove from the oven and
carefully lift out the paper and beans.
Prick the bottom of the case all over
with a fork. Return to the oven and
bake for 5 minutes more. Let the pastry
case cool slightly before filling. Turn
the oven down to 190°C/375°F/Gas 5.

6 ▲ In a small bowl, mix together
the flour and sugar using a fork.
Spread this mixture in an even layer
on the bottom of the pastry csae.

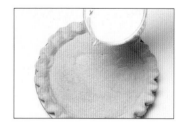

7 ▲ Stir the vanilla into the cream.
Pour the flavoured cream over the
flour and sugar mixture and gently
swirl with a fork to mix. Dot with the
butter. Sprinkle the nutmeg on top.

8 Cover the edge of the tart with foil
strips to prevent overbrowning. Set on
a baking sheet and bake until the
filling is golden brown and set to the
touch, about 45 minutes. Serve the
tart at room temperature.

Apple Maple Dumplings

SERVES 8

475g/18oz/4½ cups plain (all-purpose) flour
10ml/2 tsp salt
350g/12oz/1½ cups butter or lard, diced
90–105ml/6–7 tbsp iced water
8 firm, tart-sweet apples
1 egg white
130g/4½oz/⅔ cup granulated sugar
45ml/3 tbsp whipping cream
2.5ml/½ tsp vanilla extract
250ml/8fl oz/1 cup maple syrup
whipped cream, to serve

1 Sift the flour and salt into a large bowl. Using your fingertips, rub the butter or lard into the flour until the mixture resembles breadcrumbs. Sprinkle with 90ml/6 tbsp of the water and mix until it holds together. If it is too crumbly, add more water, 5ml/1 tsp at a time. Gather into a ball. Wrap in clear film (plastic wrap) and chill for 20 minutes.

2 Preheat oven to 220°C/425°F/Gas 7.

3 Peel the apples. Remove the cores, cutting from the stem end, without cutting through the base.

4 ▲ Roll out the pastry thinly. Cut squares almost large enough to enclose the apples. Brush the squares with egg white. Set an apple in the centre of each pastry square.

5 Combine the sugar, cream and vanilla in a small bowl. Spoon some into the hollow in each apple.

6 ▼ Pull the points of the pastry squares up around the apples and moisten the edges where they overlap. Mold the pastry around the apples, pleating the top. Do not cover the centre hollows. Crimp the edges tightly to seal.

7 Place the apples in a large greased baking dish, at least 2cm/¾in apart. Bake for 30 minutes. Lower the oven temperature to 180°C/350°F/Gas 4 and continue baking until the pastry is golden brown and the apples are tender, about 20 minutes more.

8 Transfer the dumplings to a serving dish. Mix the maple syrup with the juices in the baking dish and drizzle over the dumplings.

9 Serve the dumplings hot with whipped cream.

Apple Fritters

SERVES 4–6

165g/5½oz/1⅓ cups plain
  (all-purpose) flour

10ml/2 tsp baking powder

1.5ml/¼ tsp salt

150ml/¼ pint/⅔ cup milk

1 egg, beaten

oil for deep-frying

150g/5oz/¾ cup granulated sugar

5ml/1 tsp ground cinnamon

2 large tart-sweet apples, peeled, cored
  and cut into 5mm/¼in slices

icing (confectioners') sugar, for dusting

1 Sift the flour, baking powder and salt into a bowl. Beat in the milk and egg with a wire whisk.

2 Heat at least 7.5cm/3in oil in a heavy frying pan to 185°C/360°F.

3 ▲ Mix the granulated sugar and cinnamon in a shallow bowl or plate. Toss the apple slices in the sugar mixture to coat all over.

4 Dip the apple slices in the batter, using a fork or slotted spoon. Drain off the excess batter. Fry, in batches, in the hot oil until golden brown on both sides, about 4–5 minutes. Drain the fritters on kitchen paper.

5 ▼ Sprinkle with icing sugar, and serve hot.

Cherry Compote

SERVES 6

120ml/4fl oz/½ cup water

120ml/4fl oz/½ cup red wine

50g/2oz/¼ cup soft light brown sugar

50g/2oz/¼ cup granulated sugar

15ml/1 tbsp honey

2 × 2.5cm/1in strips of orange rind

1.5ml/¼ tsp almond extract

675g/1½lb sweet cherries, pitted

ice cream or whipped cream, to serve

1 ▼ Combine all the ingredients except the cherries in a pan. Stir over a medium heat until the sugar dissolves. Raise the heat and boil until the liquid reduces slightly.

2 ▲ Add the cherries. Bring back to the boil. Reduce the heat slightly and simmer for 8–10 minutes. If necessary, skim off any foam.

3 Leave to cool to lukewarm. Spoon warm over vanilla ice cream, or chill and serve cold with whipped cream, if you like.

~ VARIATION ~

Sour cherries may be used for the compote instead of sweet. If using sour cherries, increase the amount of the sugars to 75g/3oz/⅓ cup each, or to taste.

Apple Fritters (top), Cherry Compote

Black Walnut Layer Cake

SERVES 8

225g/8oz/2 cups self-raising (self-rising) flour

15ml/1 tbsp baking powder

2.5ml/½ tsp salt

115g/4oz/½ cup butter or margarine

200g/7oz/1 cup granulated sugar

2 eggs

5ml/1 tsp grated orange rind

5ml/1 tsp vanilla extract

115g/4oz/1 cup finely chopped black walnut pieces

175ml/6fl oz/¾ cup milk

black walnut halves, for decoration

FOR THE ICING

115g/4oz/½ cup butter

175g/6oz/¾ cup soft light brown sugar

45ml/3 tbsp maple syrup

50ml/2fl oz/¼ cup milk

200g/7oz/1¼ cups–225g/8oz/2 cups icing (confectioners') sugar, sifted

1 ▲ Grease two 20 × 5cm/8 × 2in cake tins (pans) and line each with a disk of greased baking parchment. Preheat the oven to 190°C/ 375°F/Gas 5.

2 Sift together the flour, baking powder and salt.

~ **VARIATION** ~

If black walnuts are unavailable, substitute regular walnuts, or use pecans instead.

3 ▲ Beat the butter or margarine to soften, then gradually beat in the granulated sugar until light and fluffy. Beat in the eggs, one at a time. Add the orange rind and vanilla and beat to mix well.

4 ▲ Stir in the finely chopped walnuts. Add the flour alternately with the milk, stirring only enough to blend after each addition.

5 ▲ Divide the mixture between the prepared cake tins. Bake until a skewer inserted in the centre comes out clean, about 25 minutes. Cool in the tins for 5 minutes before turning out on to a wire rack.

6 ▲ For the icing, melt the butter in a medium pan. Add the brown sugar and maple syrup and boil for 2 minutes, stirring constantly.

7 ▲ Add the milk. Bring back to the boil and stir in 25g/1oz/¼ cup of the icing sugar. Remove from the heat and leave to cool to lukewarm. Gradually beat in the remaining icing sugar. Set the pan in a bowl of iced water and stir until the icing is thick enough to spread over the cake.

8 ▲ Spread some of the icing on one of the cake layers. Set the other layer on top. Spread the remaining icing over the top and sides of the cake. Decorate with the walnut halves.

Apple Sauce Cookies

MAKES 36

90g/3½oz/½ cup granulated sugar

50g/2oz/¼ cup butter, lard or white
  cooking fat, at room temperature

175ml/6fl oz/¾ cup thick apple sauce

pinch of grated lemon rind

115g/4oz/1 cup plain (all-purpose) flour

2.5ml/½ tsp baking powder

1.5ml/¼ tsp bicarbonate of soda
  (baking soda)

1.5ml/¼ tsp salt

2.5ml/½ tsp ground cinnamon

50g/2oz/½ cup chopped walnuts

~ COOK'S TIP ~

If the apple sauce is runny, put it
in a strainer over a bowl and let it
drain for 10 minutes.

1 Preheat oven to 190°C/375°F/Gas 5.

2 In a medium bowl, beat together the
sugar and butter, lard or white cooking
fat until well mixed. Beat in the apple
sauce and lemon rind.

3 ▲ Sift the flour, baking powder,
bicarbonate of soda, salt and cinnamon
into the mixture, and stir to blend.
Fold in the chopped walnuts.

4 ▲ Drop teaspoonfuls of the mixture
on to a lightly greased baking sheet,
spacing them about 5cm/2in apart.

5 Bake the cookies in the centre of
the oven until they are golden brown,
8–10 minutes. Transfer the cookies to
a wire rack to cool.

Toffee Bars

MAKES 32

450g/1lb/2 cups soft light brown sugar

450g/1lb/2 cups butter or margarine,
  at room temperature

2 egg yolks

7.5ml/1½ tsp vanilla extract

450g/1lb/4 cups plain (all-purpose) or
  wholemeal (whole-wheat) flour

2.5ml/½ tsp salt

225g/8oz milk chocolate, broken in pieces

115g/4oz/1 cup chopped walnuts
  or pecans

1 Preheat the oven to 180°C/350°F/
Gas 4.

2 Beat together the sugar and butter
or margarine until light and fluffy.
Beat in the egg yolks and vanilla. Stir
in the flour and salt.

3 ▼ Spread the shortbread in a greased
15 × 3½ × 5cm/13 × 9 × 2in baking tin
(pan). Bake until lightly browned,
25–30 minutes. The texture will be soft.

4 ▲ Remove from the oven and
immediately place the chocolate
pieces on the hot shortbread base.
Leave until the chocolate softens, then
spread it evenly with a spatula.
Sprinkle with the nuts.

5 While still warm, cut into bars of
about 5 × 4cm/2 × 1½in.

Apple Sauce Cookies (top), Toffee Bars

THE SOUTHWEST

THE POPULAR TASTE FOR "TEX-MEX" HAS SPREAD FAR AND WIDE, BUT THE ROOTS OF THIS CUISINE ARE IN NATIVE AMERICAN HERITAGE. THE FOOD OF THIS REGION FEATURES PRODUCTS CULTIVATED BY THE ORIGINAL AMERICANS – CORN IN MANY FORMS, TOMATOES, BEANS – COMBINED WITH INFLUENCES FROM SOUTH OF THE BORDER AND FROM THE RIGOURS OF FARMING IN A DESERT.

Tortilla Soup

SERVES 4–6

15ml/1 tbsp vegetable oil

1 onion, finely chopped

1 large garlic clove, finely chopped

2 medium tomatoes, peeled, seeded, chopped

2.5ml/½ tsp salt

2.5 litres/4 pints chicken stock

1 carrot, diced

1 small courgette (zucchini), diced

1 skinless chicken breast fillet,
    cooked and shredded

40g/1½oz/¼ cup canned green chillies,
    chopped

TO GARNISH

4 corn tortillas

oil for frying

1 small ripe avocado

2 spring onions (scallions), chopped

chopped fresh coriander (cilantro)

grated Cheddar or Monterey Jack
    cheese (optional)

1 ▲ Heat the oil in a pan. Add the onion and garlic and cook over a medium heat until just softened, 5–8 minutes. Add the tomatoes and salt and cook for 5 minutes more.

2 Stir in the stock. Bring to the boil, then lower the heat and simmer, covered, for about 15 minutes.

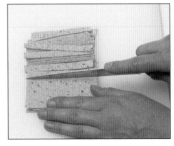

3 ▲ Meanwhile, for the garnish, trim the tortillas into squares, then cut them into strips.

4 ▲ Put a 1cm/½in layer of oil in a frying pan and heat until hot but not smoking. Add the tortilla strips, in batches, and fry until just beginning to brown, turning occasionally. Remove with a slotted spoon and drain on kitchen paper.

5 Add the carrot to the soup. Cook, covered, for 10 minutes. Add the courgette, chicken and chillies and continue cooking, uncovered, until the vegetables are just tender, about 5 minutes more.

6 Meanwhile, peel and stone (pit) the avocado. Chop into fine dice.

7 Divide the tortilla strips among four soup bowls. Sprinkle with the avocado. Ladle in the soup, then scatter spring onions and coriander on top. Serve at once, with grated cheese if you like.

Spicy Bean Soup

SERVES 6–8

175g/6oz/1 cup dried black beans, soaked overnight and drained

175g/6oz/1 cup dried kidney beans, soaked overnight and drained

2 bay leaves

90ml/6 tbsp sea salt

30ml/2 tbsp olive or vegetable oil

3 carrots, chopped

1 onion, chopped

1 celery stick

1 garlic clove, finely chopped

5ml/1 tsp ground cumin

1.5–2.5ml/¼–½ tsp cayenne pepper

2.5ml/½ tsp dried oregano

salt and pepper

75ml/2½fl oz/⅓ cup red wine

1.2 litres/2 pints beef stock

250ml/8fl oz/1 cup water

TO GARNISH

sour cream

chopped fresh coriander (cilantro)

1 ▲ Put the black beans and kidney beans in two separate pans. To each, add a bay leaf and fresh cold water to cover. Bring to the boil, then cover and simmer for 30 minutes.

2 Add half the sea salt to each pan and continue simmering until the beans are tender, about 30 minutes more. Drain and leave to cool slightly. Discard the bay leaves.

3 Heat the oil in a large flameproof casserole. Add the carrots, onion, celery and garlic and cook over a low heat, stirring, until softened, about 8–10 minutes. Stir in the cumin, cayenne, oregano and salt to taste.

4 ▼ Add the wine, stock and water and stir to mix. Add the beans. Bring to the boil, reduce the heat, then cover and simmer for about 20 minutes, stirring occasionally.

5 ▲ Transfer half the soup (including most of the solids) to a food processor or blender. Process until smooth. Return to the pan and stir to combine well.

6 Reheat the soup if necessary and taste for seasoning. Serve hot, garnished with sour cream and chopped fresh coriander.

Desert Nachos

175g/6oz blue corn tortilla chips or
   ordinary tortilla chips

30–60ml/2–4 tbsp chopped pickled
   jalapeños, according to taste

25g/1oz/⅓ cup sliced black olives

250g/8oz/2 cups grated Monterey Jack
   or Cheddar cheese

TO SERVE

guacamole

tomato salsa

sour cream

1 Preheat the oven to 180°C/350°F/
Gas 4.

2 ▲ Put the tortilla chips in a 33 ×
23cm/13 × 9in baking dish and spread
them out evenly. Sprinkle the jalapeños,
olives and cheese evenly over the
tortilla chips.

3 ▼ Place in the top of the oven
and bake until the cheese melts,
10–15 minutes. Serve the nachos at
once, with the guacamole, tomato salsa
and sour cream for dipping.

Huevos Rancheros

460g/17oz can refried beans

300ml/½ pint/1¼ cups enchilada sauce

oil for frying

4 corn tortillas

4 eggs

salt and pepper

150g/5oz/1¼ cups grated Monterey Jack
   or Cheddar cheese

1 ▼ Heat the beans in a pan. Cover
and set aside.

2 Heat the enchilada sauce in a small
pan. Cover and set aside.

3 Preheat oven to 160°C/325°F/Gas 3.

4 ▲ Put a 6mm/¼in layer of oil in a
small non-stick frying pan and heat.
When hot, add the tortillas, one at a
time, and fry until just crisp, about
30 seconds per side. Drain the tortillas
on kitchen paper and keep them warm
on a baking sheet in the oven. Discard
the oil used for frying.

5 Leave the frying pan to cool slightly,
then wipe it with kitchen paper to
remove all but a film of oil. Heat the
pan over a low heat. Break in 2 eggs
and cook until the whites are just set.
Season with salt and pepper, then
transfer to the oven to keep warm.
Repeat to cook the remaining eggs.

6 ▼ To serve, place a tortilla on
each of four plates. Spread a layer of
refried beans over each tortilla, then
top each with an egg. Spoon over the
warm enchilada sauce, then sprinkle
with the cheese. Serve hot.

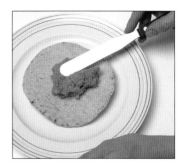

Desert Nachos (top), Huevos Rancheros

Arizona Jalapeño and Onion Quiche

SERVES 6

15ml/1 tbsp butter

2 onions, sliced

4 spring onions (scallions), cut into 1cm/½in pieces

2.5ml/½ tsp ground cumin

15–30ml/1–2 tbsp chopped canned jalapeños

4 eggs

300ml/½ pint/1¼ cups milk

2.5ml/½ tsp salt

65g/2½oz/⅔ cup grated Monterey Jack or Cheddar cheese

FOR THE PASTRY

175g/6oz/1½ cups plain (all-purpose) flour

1.5ml/¼ tsp salt

1.5ml/¼ tsp cayenne pepper

75g/3oz/6 tbsp cold butter or margarine

30–45ml/2–3 tbsp iced water

1 For the pastry, sift the flour, salt and cayenne into a bowl. Using your fingertips, rub the butter and margarine into the dry ingredients until the mixture is crumbly and resembles breadcrumbs. Sprinkle with 30ml/2 tbsp of the iced water and mix until the pastry holds together. If the pastry is too crumbly, add a little more water, 5ml/1 tsp at a time. Gather the pastry into a ball and flatten into a disk. Wrap in clear film (plastic wrap) and chill for at least 30 minutes.

2 Preheat the oven to 190°C/375°F/ Gas 5.

3 Roll the pastry out to about 3mm/⅛in thick. Use to line a 23cm/9in fluted tart tin (pan) with a removable base. Line the case with baking parchment and fill with dried beans.

4 Bake until the pastry has just set, 12–15 minutes. Remove from the oven and carefully lift out the paper and beans. Prick the bottom of the pastry case all over. Return to the oven and bake until golden, 5–8 minutes more. Leave the oven on.

5 ▲ Melt the butter in a non-stick frying pan. Add the onions and cook over a medium heat until softened, about 5 minutes. Add the spring onions and cook for 1 minute more. Stir in the cumin and jalapeños and set aside.

6 In a mixing bowl, combine the eggs, milk and salt and whisk until thoroughly blended.

7 ▲ Spoon the onion mixture into the pastry case. Sprinkle with the cheese, then pour in the egg mixture.

8 Bake until the filling is golden and set, 30–40 minutes. Serve hot or at room temperature.

San Antonio Tortilla

SERVES 4

15ml/1 tbsp vegetable oil

½ onion, sliced

1 small green (bell) pepper,
  seeded and sliced

1 garlic clove, finely chopped

1 tomato, chopped

6 black olives, chopped

3 small potatoes (about 275g/10oz
  total), cooked and sliced

50g/2oz sliced chorizo, cut into strips

15ml/1 tbsp chopped canned jalapeños,
  or to taste

50g/2oz/½ cup grated Cheddar cheese

6 large (US extra large) eggs

45ml/3 tbsp milk

2.5–6ml/½–¾ tsp salt

1.5ml/¼ tsp ground cumin

1.5ml/¼ tsp dried oregano

1.5ml/¼ tsp paprika

black pepper

1 Preheat the oven to 190°C/375°F/
Gas 5.

2 ▲ Heat the oil in a non-stick frying
pan. Add the onion, green pepper and
garlic and cook over a medium heat
until softened, 5–8 minutes.

3 Transfer the vegetables to a 23cm/9in
round non-stick springform tin (pan).
Add the tomato, olives, potatoes,
chorizo and jalapeños. Sprinkle with
the cheese and set aside.

4 ▲ In a bowl, combine the eggs and
milk and whisk until frothy. Add the
salt, cumin, oregano, paprika and
pepper to taste. Whisk to blend.

5 Pour the egg mixture into the
vegetable mixture, tilting the pan to
spread it evenly.

6 ▲ Bake until set and lightly golden,
about 30 minutes. Serve hot or cold.

Santa Fe Prawn Salad

SERVES 4

450g/1lb cooked peeled prawns

2 spring onions (scallions), chopped

30ml/2 tbsp fresh lemon juice

30ml/2 tbsp extra virgin olive oil

5ml/1 tsp salt

350g/12oz/6 cups shredded lettuce

1 large ripe avocado

225g/8oz/1 cup tomato salsa

TO GARNISH

fresh coriander (cilantro) sprigs

lime slices

1 ▲ In a bowl, combine the prawns, spring onions, lemon juice, oil and salt. Mix well and set aside.

2 ▲ Line four plates (or a large serving dish) with the shredded lettuce.

3 ▲ Halve the avocado and remove the stone (pit). With a small melon baller, scoop out balls of avocado and add to the prawn mixture. Scrape the remaining avocado flesh into the salsa and stir. Add the salsa to the prawn mixture and stir gently to blend.

4 ▲ Divide the prawn mixture among the plates, piling it up in the centre. Garnish each salad with fresh coriander sprigs and slices of lime, and serve at once.

Pinto Bean Salad

SERVES 4

260g/9½oz/1½ cups dried pinto beans, soaked overnight and drained

1 bay leaf

45ml/3 tbsp sea salt

2 ripe tomatoes, diced

4 spring onions (scallions), finely chopped

FOR THE DRESSING

50ml/2fl oz/¼ cup fresh lemon juice

5ml/1 tsp salt

pepper

90ml/6 tbsp olive oil

1 garlic clove, finely chopped

45ml/3 tbsp chopped fresh coriander (cilantro)

1 ▲ Put the beans in a large pan. Add fresh cold water to cover and the bay leaf. Bring to the boil, then cover and simmer for 30 minutes. Add the salt and continue simmering until tender, about 30 minutes more. Drain and leave to cool slightly. Discard the bay leaf.

2 ▲ For the dressing, mix the lemon juice and salt with a fork until dissolved. Gradually stir in the oil until thick. Add the garlic, coriander and pepper to taste.

3 ▲ While the beans are still warm, place them in a medium bowl. Add the dressing and toss to coat. Let the beans cool completely.

4 ▼ Add the tomatoes and spring onions and toss to coat evenly. Leave to stand for at least 30 minutes, then serve.

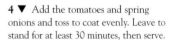

Chillies Rellenos

<u>SERVES 4</u>

8 large green (bell) peppers or fresh green chillies such as poblano

15–30ml/1–2 tbsp vegetable oil, plus more for frying

450g/1lb/4 cups grated Monterey Jack or Cheddar cheese

4 eggs, separated

75g/3oz/⅔ cup plain (all-purpose) flour

<u>FOR THE SAUCE</u>

15ml/1 tbsp vegetable oil

1 small onion, finely chopped

1.5ml/¼ tsp salt

5–10ml/1–2 tsp red pepper flakes

2.5ml/½ tsp ground cumin

250ml/8fl oz/1 cup beef or chicken stock

450g/1lb canned peeled tomatoes

1 ▲ For the sauce, heat the oil in a frying pan. Add the onion and cook over a low heat until just soft, about 8 minutes. Stir in the salt, pepper flakes, cumin, stock and tomatoes. Cover and simmer gently for 5 minutes, stirring occasionally.

2 Transfer to a food processor or blender and process until smooth. Strain into a clean pan. Taste for seasoning, and set aside.

~ COOK'S TIP ~

If necessary, work in batches, but do not coat the peppers until you are ready to fry them.

---

3 Preheat the grill (broiler).

4 ▲ Brush the peppers or chillies lightly all over with oil. Lay them on a baking sheet. Grill (broil) as close to the heat as possible until blackened all over, 5–8 minutes. Cover with a clean dish towel and set aside.

5 ▲ When cool enough to handle, remove the charred skin. Carefully slit the peppers or chillies and scoop out the seeds. If using chillies, wear rubber gloves. For less chilli-heat, gently remove the white veins.

6 ▲ With your hands, form the cheese into eight cylinders that are slightly shorter than the peppers. Place the cheese cylinders inside the peppers. Secure the slits with wooden toothpicks. Set aside.

7 ▲ Beat the egg whites until just stiff. Add the egg yolks, one at a time, beating on low speed just to incorporate them. Beat in 15ml/1 tbsp of the flour.

8 Put a 2.5cm/1in layer of oil in a frying pan. Heat until hot but not smoking. (To test, drop a scrap of batter in the oil: if the oil sizzles, it is hot enough for frying.)

9 ▲ Coat the peppers lightly in flour all over; shake off any excess. Dip into the egg batter, then place in the hot oil. Fry until brown on one side, about 2 minutes. Turn carefully and brown the other side.

10 Reheat the sauce and serve with the chillies rellenos.

~ VARIATION ~

If using peppers rather than green chillies, mix the grated cheese with 7.5–15ml/½–1 tbsp hot chilli powder for a more authentic Southwest taste.

Black Bean Burritos

SERVES 4

185g/6½oz/1 cup dried black beans, soaked overnight and drained

1 bay leaf

45ml/3 tbsp sea salt

1 small red onion, finely chopped

225g/8oz/2 cups grated Monterey Jack or Cheddar cheese

15–45ml/1–3 tbsp chopped pickled jalapeños

15ml/1 tbsp chopped fresh coriander (cilantro)

800g/1¾lb/3½ cups tomato salsa

8 flour tortillas

diced avocado, to serve

1 ▲ Place the beans in a large pan. Add fresh cold water to cover and the bay leaf. Bring to the boil, then cover and simmer for 30 minutes. Add the salt and continue simmering until tender, about 30 minutes more. Drain and leave to cool slightly. Discard the bay leaf.

2 Preheat the oven to 180°C/350°F/ Gas 4. Grease a rectangular baking dish.

3 ▲ In a bowl, combine the beans, onion, half the cheese, the jalapeños, coriander and 250g/8oz/1 cup of salsa. Stir to blend and taste for seasoning.

4 ▲ Place a tortilla on a work surface. Spread a large spoonful of the filling down the middle, then roll up to enclose the filling. Place the burrito in the prepared dish, seam side down. Repeat with the remaining tortillas.

5 ▲ Sprinkle the remaining cheese over the burritos, in a line down the middle. Bake until the cheese melts, about 15 minutes.

6 Serve the burritos at once, with the avocado and remaining salsa.

Black Bean Chilli

SERVES 6

375g/13oz/2 cups dried black beans, soaked overnight and drained

30ml/2 tbsp sea salt

30ml/2 tbsp vegetable oil

2 onions, chopped

1 green (bell) pepper, seeded and chopped

4 garlic cloves, finely chopped

900g/2lb steak mince

25ml/1½ tbsp ground cumin

2.5ml/½ tsp cayenne pepper, or to taste

12.5ml/2½ tsp paprika

30ml/2 tbsp dried oregano

5ml/1 tsp salt

45ml/3 tbsp tomato purée (paste)

675g/1½lb/3 cups chopped peeled fresh or canned tomatoes

120ml/4fl oz/½ cup red wine

1 bay leaf

TO SERVE

chopped fresh coriander (cilantro)

sour cream

grated Monterey Jack or Cheddar cheese

1 Put the beans in a large pan. Add fresh cold water to cover. Bring to the boil, then cover and simmer for 30 minutes. Add the sea salt and continue simmering until the beans are tender, about 30 minutes or longer. Drain and set aside.

2 Heat the oil in a large pan or flame-proof casserole. Add the onions and pepper. Cook the vegetables over a medium heat until just softened, about 5 minutes, stirring occasionally. Stir in the garlic and continue cooking for 1 minute more.

3 Add the mince and cook over a high heat, stirring frequently, until browned and crumbly. Reduce the heat and stir in the cumin, cayenne, paprika, oregano and salt.

4 ▼ Add the tomato purée, tomatoes, drained black beans, wine and bay leaf and stir well. Simmer for 20 minutes, stirring occasionally.

5 ▲ Taste for seasoning. Remove the bay leaf and serve at once, with chopped fresh coriander, sour cream and grated cheese on the side.

Red Snapper with Coriander Salsa

SERVES 4

4 red snapper fillets, about 175g/6oz each

25ml/1½ tbsp vegetable oil

15g/½oz/1 tbsp butter

salt and pepper

FOR THE SALSA

115g/4oz/2 cups fresh coriander
(cilantro) leaves

250ml/8fl oz/1 cup olive oil

2 garlic cloves, chopped

2 tomatoes, cored and chopped

30ml/2 tbsp fresh orange juice

15ml/1 tbsp sherry vinegar

5ml/1 tsp salt

1 ▲ For the salsa, place the coriander, oil and garlic in a food processor or blender. Process until almost smooth. Add the tomatoes and pulse on and off several times; the mixture should be slightly chunky.

2 ▲ Transfer to a bowl. Stir in the orange juice, vinegar and salt. Set the salsa aside.

3 ▲ Rinse the fish fillets and pat dry. Sprinkle on both sides with salt and pepper. Heat the oil and butter in a large non-stick frying pan. When hot, add the fish and cook until opaque throughout, 2–3 minutes on each side. Work in batches, if necessary.

4 ▲ Carefully transfer the fillets to warmed dinner plates. Top each with a spoonful of salsa. Serve additional salsa on the side.

Cornmeal-coated Gulf Prawns

SERVES 4

75g/3oz/¾ cup cornmeal

5–10ml/1–2 tsp cayenne pepper

2.5ml/½ tsp ground cumin

5ml/1 tsp salt

30ml/2 tbsp chopped fresh coriander
(cilantro) or parsley

900g/2lb large raw Gulf or king prawns
(jumbo shrimp), peeled and deveined

flour, for dredging

50ml/2fl oz/¼ cup vegetable oil

115g/4oz/1 cup grated Monterey Jack or
Cheddar cheese

TO SERVE

lime wedges

tomato salsa

1 Preheat the grill (broiler).

2 ▲ In a medium bowl, combine the cornmeal, cayenne, cumin, salt and coriander or parsley.

3 ▲ Coat the prawns lightly in flour, then dip in water and roll in the cornmeal mixture to coat.

4 ▼ Heat the oil in a non-stick frying pan. When hot, add the prawns, in batches if necessary. Cook until they are opaque throughout, 2–3 minutes on each side. Drain on kitchen paper.

5 ▲ Place the prawns in a large baking dish, or individual dishes. Sprinkle the cheese evenly over the top. Grill (broil) about 7.5cm/3in from the heat until the cheese melts, 2–3 minutes. Serve at once, with lime wedges and tomato salsa.

Galveston Chicken

<u>SERVES</u> 4

1.6kg/3½lb chicken

juice of 1 lemon

4 garlic cloves, finely chopped

15ml/1 tbsp cayenne pepper

15ml/1 tbsp paprika

15ml/1 tbsp dried oregano

2.5ml/½ tsp coarsely ground black pepper

10ml/2 tsp olive oil

5ml/1 tsp salt

~ COOK'S TIP ~

Roasting chicken in an oven that
has not been preheated produces
a particularly crispy skin.

1 ▼ With a sharp knife or poultry
shears, remove the backbone from the
chicken. Turn it breast side up. With
the heel of your hand, press down to
break the breastbone, and open the
chicken flat like a book. Insert a
skewer through the chicken, at the
thighs, to keep it flat during cooking.

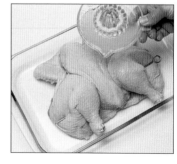

2 ▲ Place the chicken in a shallow
dish and pour over the lemon juice.

3 ▲ In a small bowl, combine the
garlic, cayenne, paprika, oregano,
pepper and oil. Mix well. Rub evenly
over the surface of the chicken.

4 Cover and leave to marinate for
2–3 hours at room temperature, or
chill overnight (return to room temperature before roasting).

5 Season the chicken with salt on
both sides. Transfer to a shallow
roasting pan.

6 Put the pan in a cold oven and set
the temperature to 200°C/400°F/Gas 6.
Roast until the chicken is done, about
1 hour, turning occasionally and basting
with the pan juices. To test if the
chicken is done, prick with a skewer:
the juices that run out should be clear.

Turkey Breasts with Tomato-Corn Salsa

SERVES 4

4 skinless turkey breast fillets, about
    175g/6oz each

30ml/2 tbsp fresh lemon juice

30ml/2 tbsp olive oil

2.5ml/½ tsp ground cumin

2.5ml/½ tsp dried oregano

5ml/1 tsp coarsely ground black pepper

salt

FOR THE SALSA

1 hot green chilli pepper

450g/1lb tomatoes, seeded and chopped

250g/9oz/1½ cups corn kernels, cooked,
    canned or thawed frozen

3 spring onions (scallions), chopped

15ml/1 tbsp chopped fresh parsley

30ml/2 tbsp chopped fresh
    coriander (cilantro)

30ml/2 tbsp fresh lemon juice

45ml/3 tbsp olive oil

5ml/1 tsp salt

1 ▲ With a meat mallet, pound the turkey fillets between two sheets of baking parchment until thin.

~ **VARIATION** ~

Use the cooked turkey, thinly sliced and combined with the salsa, as a filling for warmed flour tortillas.

2 ▲ In a shallow dish, combine the lemon juice, oil, cumin, oregano and pepper. Add the turkey and turn to coat. Cover and leave to stand for at least 2 hours, or chill overnight.

3 For the salsa, roast the chilli over a gas flame, holding it with tongs, until charred on all sides. (Alternatively, char the skin under the grill/broiler.) Leave to cool for 5 minutes. Wearing rubber gloves, carefully rub off the charred skin. For a less hot flavour, discard the seeds. Chop the chilli finely and place in a bowl.

4 ▲ Add the remaining salsa ingredients to the chilli and toss well to blend. Set aside.

5 Remove the turkey from the marinade. Season lightly on both sides with salt to taste.

6 Heat a ridged frying pan. When hot, add the turkey breasts and cook until browned, about 3 minutes. Turn and cook the meat on the other side until it is cooked through, 3–4 minutes more. Serve the turkey at once, accompanied by the salsa.

Spicy New Mexico Pork Stew

SERVES 6

250ml/8fl oz/1 cup water

15ml/1 tbsp tomato purée (paste)

4 garlic cloves, finely chopped

10ml/2 tsp dried oregano

12.5ml/2½ tsp ground cumin

10ml/2 tsp salt

15–45ml/1–3 tbsp red pepper flakes

900g/4lb boneless pork shoulder, cubed

2 onions, thickly sliced

warm flour tortillas, for serving

1 In a large casserole, combine the water, tomato purée, garlic, oregano, cumin and salt. Add red pepper flakes to taste and stir to mix.

2 ▲ Add the pork cubes and toss to coat them evenly. Cover and allow to marinate for 6–8 hours, or overnight, in the refrigerator.

3 Preheat oven to 150°C/300°F/Gas 2.

4 ▼ Cover the casserole and put in the oven. Cook for 1½ hours. Add the onions and cook for 1½ hours more. Serve with flour tortillas.

Turkey and Chorizo Tacos

SERVES 4

15ml/1 tbsp vegetable oil

450g/1lb turkey mince

5ml/1 tsp salt

5ml/1 tsp ground cumin

12 taco shells

75g/3oz chorizo, finely chopped

3 spring onions (scallions), chopped

2 tomatoes, chopped

150g/5oz/2½ cups shredded lettuce

250g/8oz/2 cups grated Monterey Jack or Cheddar cheese

TO SERVE

tomato salsa

guacamole

~ VARIATION ~

For Chicken Tacos, use finely chopped chicken instead of turkey.

1 Preheat oven to 180°C/350°F/Gas 4.

2 ▲ Heat the oil in a non-stick frying pan. Add the turkey, salt and cumin and sauté over a medium heat until the turkey is cooked through, 5–8 minutes. Stir frequently to prevent large lumps from forming.

3 Meanwhile, arrange the taco shells in one layer on a large baking sheet and heat in the oven for about 10 minutes, or according to the directions on the packet.

4 Add the chorizo and spring onions to the turkey and stir to mix. Cook until just warmed through, stirring the mixture occasionally.

5 ▲ To assemble each taco, place 1–2 spoonfuls of the turkey mixture in the bottom of a warmed taco shell. Top with a generous sprinkling of chopped tomato, shredded lettuce and grated cheese.

6 Serve at once, with tomato salsa and guacamole.

Spicy New Mexico Pork Stew (top), Turkey and Chorizo Tacos

Pork Chops with Sour Green Chilli Salsa

SERVES 4

30ml/2 tbsp vegetable oil
15ml/1 tbsp fresh lemon juice
10ml/2 tsp ground cumin
5ml/1 tsp dried oregano
salt and pepper
8 pork loin chops, about 2cm/¾in thick

FOR THE SALSA

2 hot green chilli peppers
2 green (bell) peppers, seeded and chopped
1 tomato, peeled and seeded
½ onion, coarsely chopped
4 spring onions (scallions)
1 pickled jalapeño, stem removed
30ml/2 tbsp olive oil
30ml/2 tbsp fresh lime juice
45ml/3 tbsp cider vinegar
5ml/1 tsp salt

1 In a small bowl, combine the vegetable oil, lemon juice, cumin and oregano. Add pepper to taste and stir to blend.

2 ▼ Arrange the pork chops in one layer in a shallow dish. Brush each with the oil mixture on both sides. Cover and leave to stand for 2–3 hours, or chill overnight.

3 ▲ For the salsa, roast the chillies over a gas flame, holding them with tongs, until charred on all sides. (Alternatively, char the skins under the grill/broiler.) Leave to cool for 5 minutes. Wearing rubber gloves, remove the charred skin. For a milder flavour, discard the seeds.

4 Place the chillies in a food processor or blender. Add the remaining salsa ingredients. Process until finely chopped but do not purée.

5 Transfer the salsa to a heavy pan and simmer for 15 minutes, stirring occasionally. Set aside.

6 ▲ Season the pork chops. Heat a ridged frying pan. (Alternatively, preheat the grill/broiler.) When hot, add the pork chops and cook until browned, about 5 minutes. Turn and continue cooking until done, 5–7 minutes more. Work in batches, if necessary.

7 Serve at once, with the sour green chilli salsa.

Pork Fajitas

SERVES 6

juice of 3 limes

90ml/6 tbsp olive oil

5ml/1 tsp dried oregano

5ml/1 tsp ground cumin

2.5ml/½ tsp red pepper flakes

675g/1½lb pork tenderloin, cut across into 7.5cm/3in pieces

salt and pepper

2 large onions, halved and thinly sliced

1 large green (bell) pepper, seeded and thinly sliced lengthways

TO SERVE

12–15 flour tortillas, warmed

tomato salsa

guacamole

sour cream

1 ▲ In a shallow dish, combine the lime juice, 45ml/3 tbsp of the oil, the oregano, cumin and red pepper flakes and mix well. Add the pork pieces and turn to coat. Cover and leave to stand for 1 hour, or chill overnight.

2 Remove the pieces of pork from the marinade. Pat them dry and season with salt and pepper.

3 Heat a ridged frying pan. When hot, add the pork and cook over a high heat, turning occasionally, until browned on all sides and cooked through, about 10–12 minutes.

4 ▼ Meanwhile, heat the remaining oil in a large frying pan. Add the onions and pepper. Stir in 2.5ml/½ tsp salt and cook until the vegetables are very soft, about 15 minutes. Stir occasionally. Remove from the heat and set aside.

5 ▲ Slice the pork pieces into thin strips. Add to the onion mixture and reheat briefly if necessary.

6 Spoon a little of the pork mixture on to each tortilla. Add salsa, guacamole and sour cream, and roll up. Alternatively, the fajitas may be assembled at the table.

Lamb Stew with Cornmeal Dumplings

SERVES 6

15ml/1 tbsp vegetable oil

1 large onion, chopped

1 large celery stick, chopped

1 red (bell) pepper, seeded and chopped

675g/1½lb boneless lamb, cubed

5ml/1 tsp salt, or to taste

3 medium tomatoes, cored and chopped

5ml/1 tsp ground cumin

pinch of ground cinnamon

1.5ml/¼ tsp cayenne, or to taste

1.2 litres/2 pints/5 cups beef stock

2 courgettes (zucchini), about 225g/8oz, quartered and chopped

FOR THE DUMPLINGS

115g/4oz/1 cup cornmeal

30ml/2 tbsp plain (all-purpose) flour

10ml/2 tsp baking powder

2.5ml/½ tsp salt

1 large (US extra large) egg, beaten

30ml/2 tbsp melted butter

75ml/2½fl oz/⅓ cup milk

1 Heat the oil in a large flameproof casserole. Add the onion and celery and cook over a medium heat until just soft, about 5 minutes.

2 ▲ Add the pepper, lamb and salt. Cook until the cubes of lamb are browned, 5–7 minutes more. Stir to brown them evenly.

3 Stir in the tomatoes, spices and stock. Bring to the boil, skimming off any foam that rises to the surface. Reduce the heat, cover and simmer gently for 25 minutes. From time to time, skim off any surface fat.

4 Meanwhile, for the dumplings, heat about 5cm/2in water in the bottom of a steamer.

5 ▲ Combine the cornmeal, flour, baking powder and salt in a large bowl. Make a well in the centre and add the egg, butter and milk. Stir with a fork until blended.

6 With your hands, shape the mixture into six balls, each about 5cm/2in in diameter.

7 ▲ When the water in the steamer is hot, place the dumplings in the steamer basket. Cover and steam for about 20 minutes. (If necessary, add boiling water to replenish the bottom of the steamer.)

8 About 5 minutes before the stew has finished cooking, add the courgette and stir to mix.

9 Ladle the stew into shallow bowls. Place a dumpling in the centre of each and serve at once.

Tamale Pie

SERVES 8

115g/4oz bacon, chopped

1 onion, finely chopped

450g/1lb lean steak mince

10–15ml/2–3 tsp chilli powder

5ml/1 tsp salt

300g/11oz peeled fresh or canned tomatoes

25g/1oz/⅓ cup chopped black olives

175g/6oz/1 cup corn kernels, freshly cooked, canned or thawed frozen

120ml/4fl oz/½ cup sour cream

115g/4oz/1 cup grated Monterey Jack cheese

FOR THE TAMALE CRUST

250–300ml/8–10fl oz/1–1¼ cups chicken stock

salt and pepper

175g/6 oz/1½ cups cornmeal

75g/3 oz/6 tbsp margarine or lard

2.5ml/½ tsp baking powder

50ml/2fl oz/¼ cup milk

1 Preheat the oven to 190°C/375°F/ Gas 5.

2 Cook the bacon in a large frying pan until the fat is rendered, 2–3 minutes. Pour off the excess fat, leaving 15–30ml/ 1–2 tbsp. Add the onion and cook until just softened, about 5 minutes.

3 ▲ Add the beef, chilli powder and salt and cook for 5 minutes, stirring to break up the meat. Stir in the tomatoes and cook for 5 minutes more, breaking them up with a spoon.

4 ▲ Add the olives, corn and sour cream and mix well. Transfer to a 38cm/15in long rectangular or oval baking dish. Set aside.

5 For the crust, bring the stock to the boil in a pan; season it with salt and pepper if necessary.

6 In a food processor, combine the cornmeal, margarine or lard, baking powder and milk. Process until combined. With the machine on, gradually pour in the hot stock until a smooth, thick mixture is obtained. If the mixture is too thick to spread, add additional hot stock or water, a little at a time.

7 Pour the mixture over the top of the beef mixture, spreading it evenly with a metal spatula.

8 Bake until the top is just browned, about 20 minutes. Sprinkle the surface evenly with the grated cheese and continue baking until melted and bubbling, 10–15 minutes more. Serve at once.

Beef Enchiladas

SERVES 4

900g/2lb chuck steak

15ml/1 tbsp vegetable oil,
  plus more for frying

5ml/1 tsp salt

5ml/1 tsp dried oregano

2.5ml/½ tsp ground cumin

1 onion, quartered

2 garlic cloves, crushed

1 litre/1¾pints/4 cups enchilada sauce

12 corn tortillas

115g/4oz/1 cup grated Monterey Jack cheese

TO SERVE

1 chopped spring onion (scallion)

sour cream

1 Preheat oven to 160°C/325°F/Gas 3.

2 ▲ Place the meat on a sheet of foil. Rub all over with the oil. Sprinkle both sides with the salt, oregano and cumin and rub in well. Add the onion and garlic. Top with another sheet of foil and roll up to seal the edges, leaving room for some steam expansion during cooking.

~ COOK'S TIP ~

Allow extra tortillas because some will break when dipping in the oil or sauce.

3 ▲ Place in a baking dish. Bake until the meat is tender enough to shred, about 3 hours. Remove the meat from the foil and shred with a fork. (This can be prepared 1–2 days in advance.)

4 ▲ Add 120ml/4fl oz/½ cup of the enchilada sauce to the beef. Stir well. Spoon a thin layer of enchilada sauce on the bottom of a rectangular baking dish, or into four individual baking dishes.

5 ▲ Place the remaining enchilada sauce in a frying pan and warm gently.

6 ▲ Put a 1cm/½in layer of vegetable oil in a second frying pan and heat until hot but not smoking. With tongs, lower a tortilla into the oil; the temperature is correct if it just sizzles. Cook for 2 seconds, then turn and cook the other side for 2 seconds. Lift out, drain over the frying pan, and then transfer to the frying pan of sauce. Dip into the sauce just to coat both sides.

7 ▲ Transfer the softened tortilla immediately to a plate. Spread 2–3 spoonfuls of the beef mixture down the centre of the tortilla. Roll up and place seam-side down in the prepared dish. Repeat the process for the remaining tortillas.

8 Spoon the remaining sauce from the frying pan over the enchiladas, spreading it to the ends. Sprinkle the cheese down the centre.

9 Bake until the cheese just melts, 10–15 minutes. Sprinkle with chopped spring onions and serve at once, with sour cream on the side.

Lone Star Steak and Potato Dinner

SERVES 4

45ml/3 tbsp olive oil

5 large garlic cloves, finely chopped

5ml/1 tsp coarsely ground black pepper

2.5ml/½ tsp ground allspice

5ml/1 tsp ground cumin

2.5ml/½ tsp chilli powder

10ml/2 tsp dried oregano

15ml/1 tbsp cider vinegar

4 boneless sirloin steaks,
about 2cm/¾in thick

salt

FOR THE POTATOES

50ml/2fl oz/¼ cup vegetable oil

1 onion, chopped

5ml/1 tsp salt

900g/2lb potatoes, boiled and diced

30–75ml/2–5 tbsp chopped canned green
chillies, according to taste

TO SERVE

tomato salsa

freshly cooked corn on the cob (optional)

1 ▲ Heat the olive oil in a heavy frying pan. When hot, add the garlic and cook, stirring often, until tender and just brown, about 3 minutes; do not let the garlic burn.

2 Transfer the garlic and oil to a shallow dish large enough to hold the steaks in one layer.

3 ▲ Add the pepper, spices, herbs and vinegar to the garlic and stir to blend thoroughly. If necessary, add just enough water to obtain a moderately thick paste.

4 ▲ Add the steaks to the dish and turn to coat evenly on both sides with the spice mixture. Cover and leave to stand for 2 hours, or chill the steaks overnight. (Bring them back to room temperature before cooking.)

~ **VARIATION** ~

The steaks can also be cooked on a barbecue (charcoal grill). Prepare the fire, and when the coals are glowing red and covered with grey ash, spread them in a single layer. Cook the steaks in the centre of an oiled grill (broiling) rack set about 13cm/5in above the coals for 1 minute per side to sear them. Move them away from the centre and cook for 10–12 minutes longer for medium rare, turning once.

5 ▲ For the potatoes, heat the oil in a large non-stick frying pan. Add the onion and salt. Cook over a medium heat until softened, about 5 minutes. Add the potatoes and chillies. Cook, stirring occasionally, until well browned, 15–20 minutes.

6 ▲ Season the steaks on both sides with salt to taste. Heat a ridged frying pan. When hot, add the steaks and cook, turning once, until done to your taste. Allow about 2 minutes on each side for medium-rare, and 3–4 minutes for well done.

7 ▲ If necessary, briefly reheat the potatoes. Serve at once, with the tomato salsa and corn, if using.

Guacamole

MAKES 475ML/16FL OZ/2 CUPS

3 large ripe avocados

3 spring onions (scallions), finely chopped

1 garlic clove, finely chopped

15ml/1 tbsp olive oil

15ml/1 tbsp sour cream

2.5ml/½ tsp salt

30ml/2 tbsp fresh lemon or lime juice

1 ▲ Halve the avocados and remove the stones (pits). Peel the halves. Put the avocado flesh in a large bowl.

2 ▲ With a fork, mash the avocado flesh coarsely.

3 Add the spring onions, garlic, olive oil, sour cream, salt and lemon or lime juice. Mash until well blended, but do not overwork the mixture. Small chunks of avocado should still remain. Taste the guacamole and adjust the seasoning if necessary, with more salt or lemon or lime juice.

4 ▼ Transfer to a serving bowl. Serve at once.

~ COOK'S TIP ~

Guacamole does not keep well, but, if necessary, it can be stored in the refrigerator for a few hours. Cover the surface with clear film (plastic wrap) to prevent discolouring.

Tomato Salsa

MAKES 900ML/1½ PINTS/3¾ CUPS

1 hot green chilli pepper, seeded if desired, chopped

1 garlic clove

½ red onion, coarsely chopped

3 spring onions (scallions), chopped

15g/½oz/¼ cup fresh coriander (cilantro) leaves

675g/1½lb ripe tomatoes, seeded and coarsely chopped

1–3 canned green chillies

15ml/1 tbsp olive oil

30ml/2 tbsp fresh lime or lemon juice

2.5ml/½ tsp salt, or to taste

30–45ml/2–3 tbsp tomato juice or cold cold water

1 Place the green chilli, garlic, red onion, spring onions and coriander in a food processor or blender. Process until finely chopped.

2 ▼ Add the tomatoes, canned chillies, olive oil, lime or lemon juice, salt and tomato juice or water. Pulse on and off until just chopped; the salsa should be chunky.

3 ▲ Transfer to a bowl and taste for seasoning. Leave to stand for at least 30 minutes before serving. This salsa is best served the day it is made.

~ COOK'S TIP ~

For less heat, remove the seeds from the fresh and canned chillies.

Guacamole (top), Tomato Salsa

Tomato Rice

SERVES 4

475ml/16fl oz/2 cups unsalted chicken
　　or beef stock

7.5ml/1½ tbsp vegetable oil

1 small onion, finely chopped

200g/7oz/1 cup long grain rice

5ml/1 tsp salt

2.5ml/½ tsp ground cumin

1 tomato, peeled, seeded and chopped

15ml/1 tbsp tomato purée (paste)

15ml/1 tbsp chopped fresh
　　coriander (cilantro)

1 Place the stock in a pan and heat until just simmering. Remove from the heat, cover and set aside.

2 ▼ Heat the oil in a large heavy pan. Add the onion and rice and cook over a medium heat until the onion is just softened, about 5 minutes. Stir in the salt, cumin, tomato and tomato purée and then cook for 1 minute more, stirring frequently.

3 ▲ Gradually add the warm stock, stirring to blend. Bring to the boil, then lower the heat, cover and cook until the rice is tender and all the liquid is absorbed, 30–40 minutes.

4 Fluff the rice with a fork and stir in the coriander. Serve at once.

Enchilada Sauce

MAKES ABOUT 1.3 LITRES/2¼ PINTS/6 CUPS

4 x 450g/16oz cans peeled plum
　　tomatoes, drained

3 garlic cloves, coarsely chopped

1 onion, coarsely chopped

30–60ml/2–4 tbsp ground red chilli

5ml/1 tsp cayenne pepper, or to taste

5ml/1 tsp ground cumin

2.5ml/½ tsp dried oregano

2.5ml/½ tsp salt

1 ▼ Place the tomatoes, garlic and onion in a food processor or blender. Process until smooth.

2 Pour and scrape the mixture into a heavy pan.

~ COOK'S TIP ~

Ground red chilli is not the same thing as chilli powder. If ground red chilli is unavailable, use hot red pepper flakes and strain the sauce before using.

3 ▲ Add the remaining ingredients and stir to blend. Bring to the boil, stirring occasionally. Boil for 2–3 minutes. Reduce the heat, cover and simmer for 15 minutes.

4 Dilute with 120–250ml/4–8fl oz/ ½–1 cup water, as necessary, to obtain a pouring consistency. Taste for seasoning; if a hotter sauce is wanted, add more cayenne, not ground chilli.

Tomato Rice (top), Enchilada Sauce

Navajo Fried Bread

MAKES 8 BREAD ROUNDS

225g/8oz/2 cups plain (all-purpose) flour

10ml/2 tsp baking powder

2.5ml/½ tsp salt

250ml/8fl oz/1 cup lukewarm water

oil for frying

1 Sift the flour, baking powder and salt into a bowl. Pour in the water and stir quickly with a fork until the dough gathers into a ball.

2 ▼ With floured hands, gently knead the dough by rolling it around the bowl. Do not overknead; the dough should be very soft.

3 ▲ Divide the dough into eight pieces. With floured hands, pat each piece into a round about 13cm/5in in diameter. Place the rounds on a floured baking sheet.

4 Put a 2.5cm/1in layer of oil in a heavy frying pan and heat until hot but not smoking. To test the temperature, drop in a small piece of dough; if it bubbles at once, the oil is ready.

5 ▲ Add the dough rounds to the hot oil and press down with a slotted spoon to submerge them. Release the dough and cook until puffed and golden on both sides, 3–5 minutes total, turning for even browning. Fry in batches, if necessary.

6 Drain the bread on kitchen paper and serve at once. They are good as an accompaniment for chilli or with grated cheese and an assortment of southwestern salsas. (Fried bread will not keep.)

Bean Dip

MAKES 750ML/1¼ PINTS/3 CUPS

275g/10oz/1½ cups dried pinto beans,
  soaked overnight and drained

1 bay leaf

45ml/3 tbsp sea salt

15ml/1 tbsp vegetable oil

1 small onion, sliced

1 garlic clove, finely chopped

2–4 canned hot green chillies (optional)

75ml/2½fl oz/⅓ cup sour cream,
  plus more for garnishing

2.5ml/½ tsp ground cumin

hot pepper sauce

15ml/1 tbsp chopped fresh
  coriander (cilantro)

tortilla chips, to serve

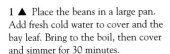

1 ▲ Place the beans in a large pan.
Add fresh cold water to cover and the
bay leaf. Bring to the boil, then cover
and simmer for 30 minutes.

2 Add the sea salt and continue
simmering until the beans are tender,
about 30 minutes or more.

3 Drain the beans, reserving 120ml/
4fl oz/½ cup of the cooking liquid. Leave
to cool slightly. Discard the bay leaf.

4 Heat the oil in a non-stick frying pan.
Add the onion and garlic and cook
over a low heat until just softened,
8–10 minutes, stirring occasionally.

5 ▲ Place the beans, onion mixture,
chillies, if using, and the reserved
cooking liquid in a food processor or
blender. Process until the mixture
resembles a coarse purée.

6 ▼ Transfer to a bowl and stir in the
sour cream, cumin and hot pepper
sauce to taste. Stir in the coriander,
garnish with sour cream and serve
warm, with tortilla chips.

Chocolate Cinnamon Cake with Banana Sauce

115g/4oz semisweet chocolate, chopped

115g/4oz/½ cup unsalted butter,
　at room temperature

15ml/1 tbsp instant coffee powder

5 eggs, separated

200g/7oz/1 cup granulated sugar

115g/4oz/1 cup plain (all-purpose) flour

10ml/2 tsp ground cinnamon

FOR THE SAUCE

4 ripe bananas

50g/2oz/¼ cup soft light brown sugar

15ml/1 tbsp fresh lemon juice

175ml/6fl oz/¾ cup whipping cream

15ml/1 tbsp rum (optional)

1 Preheat the oven to 180°C/350°F/
Gas 4. Grease a 20cm/8in round cake
tin (pan).

2 ▲ Combine the chocolate and
butter in the top of a double boiler or
in a heatproof bowl set over hot water.
Stir until melted. Remove from the
heat and stir in the coffee. Set aside.

3 Beat the egg yolks with the
granulated sugar until thick and
lemon-coloured. Add the chocolate
mixture and beat on low speed just to
blend the mixtures evenly.

4 Sift together the flour and
cinnamon into a bowl.

5 ▲ In another bowl, beat the egg
whites until they hold stiff peaks.

6 ▲ Fold a dollop of whites into the
chocolate mixture to lighten it. Fold in
the remaining whites in threee batches,
alternating with the sifted flour.

7 ▲ Pour the mixture into the
prepared tin. Bake until a skewer
inserted in the centre comes out clean,
40–50 minutes. Turn out the cake on
to a wire rack.

8 Preheat the broiler (grill).

9 ▲ For the sauce, slice the bananas
into a shallow, heatproof dish. Add
the brown sugar and lemon juice and
stir to blend. Place under the grill
(broiler) and cook, stirring occasionally,
until the sugar is caramelized and
bubbling, about 8 minutes.

10 ▲ Transfer the bananas to a bowl
and mash with a fork until almost
smooth. Stir in the cream and rum, if
using. Serve the cake and sauce warm.

~ **VARIATION** ~

For a special occasion, top the cake
slices with a scoop of ice cream
(rum and raisin, chocolate or vanilla)
before adding the banana sauce.
With this addition, the dessert
will make at least 8 portions.

Mexican Hot Fudge Sundaes

Serves 4

600ml/1 pint vanilla ice cream

600ml/1 pint coffee ice cream

2 large ripe bananas, sliced

whipped cream

toasted sliced almonds

For the sauce

50ml/2fl oz/¼ cup soft light brown sugar

185g/6½oz/½ cup light corn syrup

45ml/3 tbsp strong black coffee

5ml/1 tsp ground cinnamon

150g/5oz bittersweet chocolate,
   broken up

75ml/2½fl oz/⅓ cup whipping cream

45ml/3 tbsp coffee liqueur (optional)

1 ▼ For the sauce, combine the brown sugar, corn syrup, coffee and cinnamon in a heavy pan. Bring to the boil. Boil the mixture, stirring constantly, for about 5 minutes.

2 ▲ Remove from the heat and stir in the chocolate. When melted and smooth, stir in the cream and liqueur, if using. Leave the sauce to cool just to lukewarm, or, if made ahead, reheat gently while assembling the sundaes.

3 ▲ Fill sundae dishes with one scoop each of vanilla and coffee ice cream.

4 ▲ Arrange the bananas on the top of each dish. Pour the warm sauce over the bananas, then top each sundae with a generous rosette of whipped cream. Top with toasted almonds and serve at once.

New Mexico Christmas Biscochitos

MAKES 24

175g/6oz/1½ cups plain
(all-purpose) flour

5ml/1 tsp baking powder

pinch of salt

50g/2oz/½ cup unsalted butter, softened

90g/3½oz/½ cup granulated sugar

1 egg

5ml/1 tsp whole aniseed

15ml/1 tbsp brandy

50g/2oz/¼ cup granulated sugar mixed
with 2.5ml/½ tsp ground cinnamon,
for sprinkling

1 Sift together the flour, baking powder and salt. Set aside.

2 ▲ In a bowl, beat the butter with the sugar until soft and fluffy. Add the egg, aniseed and brandy and beat until incorporated. Fold in the dry ingredients just until blended to a dough. Chill for 30 minutes.

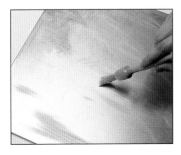

3 ▲ Preheat the oven to 180°C/350°F/ Gas 4. Grease two baking sheets.

4 On a lightly floured surface, roll out the chilled biscuit essential to about 3mm/⅛in thickness.

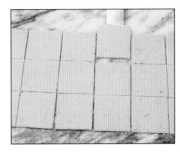

5 ▲ With a cutter, pastry wheel or knife, cut the mixture into squares, diamonds or other shapes. The traditional shape for biscochitos is a fleur-de-lis.

6 ▲ Place on the prepared baking sheets and sprinkle lightly with the cinnamon sugar.

7 Bake until just barely golden, about 10 minutes. Cool on the sheet for 5 minutes before transferring to a wire rack to cool completely. The biscuits can be kept in an airtight container for up to 1 week.

Pueblo Pastelitos

MAKES 16

450g/1lb/2 cups dried fruit, such as apricots or prunes

115g/4oz/½ cup soft light brown sugar

65g/2½oz/½ cup raisins

50g/2oz/½ cup pine nuts or chopped almonds

2.5ml/½ tsp ground cinnamon

oil for frying

45ml/3 tbsp granulated sugar mixed with 5ml/1 tsp ground cinnamon, for sprinkling

FOR THE PASTRY

225g/8oz/2 cups plain (all-purpose) flour

1.5ml/¼ tsp baking powder

1.5ml/¼ tsp salt

10ml/2 tsp granulated sugar

50g/2oz/¼ cup unsalted butter, chilled

25g/1oz/2 tbsp lard or white cooking fat

60–75ml/4–5 tbsp iced water

1 ▲ For the pastry, sift the flour, baking powder, salt and sugar into a bowl. With a pastry blender, cut in the butter until the mixture resembles breadcrumbs, or rub in with your fingertips. Sprinkle with 60ml/4 tbsp of the iced water and mix until the pastry holds together. If the pastry is too crumbly, add a little more water, 5ml/1 tsp at a time.

2 Gather the pastry into a ball and flatten into a disk. Wrap the pastry in clear film (plastic wrap) and chill for at least 30 minutes.

3 ▲ Place the dried fruit in a medium pan and add cold water to cover. Bring to the boil, then simmer gently until the fruit is soft enough to purée, about 30 minutes.

4 ▲ Drain the fruit and place in a food processor or blender. Process until smooth. Return the fruit purée to the pan. Add the brown sugar and cook, stirring constantly, until thick, about 5 minutes. Remove from the heat and stir in the raisins, pine nuts or almonds and cinnamon. Allow the mixture to cool.

5 Roll out the chilled pastry to about 3mm/⅛in thick. Stamp out rounds with a 10cm/4in pastry (cookie) cutter. (Roll and cut out in two batches if it is more convenient.)

~ **COOK'S TIP** ~

If you prefer, the pastry and the filling can both be made up to 2 days in advance and chilled.

6 ▲ Place a spoonful of the fruit filling in the centre of each round.

7 ▲ Moisten the edge with a brush dipped in water, then fold over the dough to form a half-moon shape. With a fork, crimp the rounded edge.

8 ▲ Put a 1cm/½in layer of oil in a heavy frying pan and heat until hot but not smoking. (To test, drop a scrap of dough in the oil; if the oil sizzles, it is hot enough.) Add the pastelitos, a few at a time, and fry until golden on both sides, about 1½ minutes per side.

9 Drain briefly on kitchen paper, then sprinkle with the cinnamon sugar. Serve the pastelitos warm.

Flan

SERVES 8–10

800ml/1⅓ pints/3½ cups milk

120ml/4fl oz/½ cup whipping cream

200g/7oz/1 cup granulated sugar

1 cinnamon stick

8 large (US extra large) eggs

5ml/1 tsp vanilla extract

FOR THE CARAMEL

130g/4½oz/⅔ cup granulated sugar

50ml/2fl oz/¼ cup water

1 In a medium pan, combine the milk, cream, sugar and cinnamon. Scald over a medium heat, stirring. Remove, cover and leave to stand for 30 minutes.

2 For the caramel, combine the sugar and water in a small, heavy pan over medium-high heat.

3 Bring to the boil, then simmer until the syrup begins to colour; do not stir. When the syrup is a deep golden brown, dip the base of the pan in cold water to stop it cooking.

4 ▲ Quickly pour the caramel syrup into a 3 litre/5 pint/2½ quart dish and tilt the dish to coat the bottom evenly.

5 Preheat oven to 180°C/350°F/Gas 4.

6 ▲ Reheat the milk mixture just to warm. Remove the cinnamon stick.

7 In a large bowl, combine the eggs and vanilla and mix together. Pour the milk mixture over the egg mixture, stirring constantly.

8 ▲ Place the caramel-coated dish in a large baking dish and add just enough hot water to come about 5cm/2in up the side of the dish. Pour the egg mixture through a strainer into the dish. Cover with foil.

9 Bake until the custard is just set, 40–50 minutes. Leave to cool in the water, then chill for at least 4 hours.

10 To turn out, run a knife around the inside of the dish. Place an inverted plate on top and flip over to release the flan. Scrape any remaining caramel on to the flan. Serve cold.

Southwestern Rice Pudding

SERVES 4–6

40g/1½oz/¼ cup raisins

475ml/16fl oz/2 cups water

200g/7oz/1 cup short-grain rice

1 cinnamon stick

25g/1oz/2 tbsp granulated sugar

475ml/16fl oz/2 cups milk

250ml/8fl oz/1 cup canned sweetened
   coconut cream

2.5ml/½ tsp vanilla extract

15ml/1 tbsp butter

25g/1oz/⅓ cup grated fresh coconut

ground cinnamon, for sprinkling

1 ▲ Put the raisins in a small bowl
and add water to cover. Leave to soak.

2 ▲ In a medium pan, bring the
measurement water to the boil. Add
the rice, cinnamon stick and sugar and
stir. Return to the boil, then lower the
heat, cover and simmer gently until
the liquid is absorbed, 15–20 minutes.

3 ▼ Meanwhile, combine the milk,
coconut cream and vanilla in a bowl.
Drain the raisins.

4 Remove the cinnamon stick from
the pan. Add the milk mixture and
drained raisins to the rice and stir to
mix. Continue cooking, covered and
stirring often, until the mixture is just
thick, about 20 minutes. Do not
overcook the rice.

5 Preheat the grill (broiler).

6 Transfer the mixture to a heatproof
serving dish. Dot with the butter and
sprinkle the grated coconut evenly
over the surface. Grill (broil) about
13cm/5in from the heat until the top is
just browned, 3–5 minutes. Sprinkle
with cinnamon. Serve warm or cold.

CALIFORNIA

TRENDS, CULINARY AND OTHERWISE, SEEM TO BEGIN HERE. THE LIFESTYLE – WEST COAST INFORMALITY, WITH ITS EMPHASIS ON OUTDOOR LIVING AND DINING – DICTATES A UNIQUE CUISINE. FOOD GURUS AND THEIR BOUTIQUE FARMS BRING DIVERSE AGRICULTURAL PRODUCTS INCLUDING FRUIT, BERRIES, NUTS, AVOCADOS AND ARTICHOKES TO OUR TABLES YEAR ROUND, AND CALIFORNIA WINE IS APPRECIATED WORLDWIDE.

Tomato Sandwiches with Olive Mayonnaise

SERVES 6

1 garlic clove, finely chopped

30ml/2 tbsp olive oil

5ml/1 tsp red wine vinegar

2 beefsteak tomatoes

25g/1oz/½ cup fresh basil leaves or
 parsley, chopped

1.5ml/¼ tsp salt

black pepper

7 brine-cured black olives, pitted and
 finely chopped

90ml/6 tbsp mayonnaise

12 slices of sourdough bread,
 lightly toasted

6 large lettuce leaves

1 ▼ Combine the garlic, oil and vinegar in a small bowl and mix together. Alternatively, shake the ingredients in a screwtop jar until blended. Set the dressing aside.

2 ▲ Core the tomatoes. With a sharp knife, cut six shallow lengthways slits in the skin of each to make the tomatoes easier to eat; do not cut too deeply into the flesh. Cut the tomatoes crossways into thin slices.

3 Place the tomato slices in a shallow dish. Add the oil and vinegar dressing, basil or parsley, salt and pepper to taste. Leave to marinate for at least 30 minutes.

4 ▲ In another bowl, stir together the olives and mayonnaise.

5 ▲ Spread six slices of bread with the olive mayonnaise. Arrange the tomato slices on top and drizzle over any remaining dressing from the bowl. Top each with a lettuce leaf. Cover with the remaining bread and serve.

Gazpacho

SERVES 4

½ cucumber (about 225g/8oz),
    coarsely chopped

½ green (bell) pepper, seeded and
    coarsely chopped

½ red (bell) pepper, seeded and
    coarsely chopped

1 large tomato, coarsely chopped

2 spring onions (scallions), chopped

hot pepper sauce (optional)

45ml/3 tbsp chopped fresh parsley or
    coriander (cilantro)

croutons, for serving

FOR THE SOUP BASE

450g/1lb ripe tomatoes, peeled, seeded
    and chopped

15ml/1 tbsp tomato ketchup

30ml/2 tbsp tomato purée (paste)

1.5ml/¼ tsp granulated sugar

3.5ml/¾ tsp salt

5ml/1 tsp pepper

50ml/2fl oz/¼ cup sherry vinegar

175ml/6fl oz/¾ cup olive oil

350ml/12fl oz/1½ cups tomato juice

2 Add the tomato ketchup, tomato purée, sugar, salt, pepper, vinegar and oil and pulse on and off three or four times, just to blend. Transfer to a large bowl. Stir in the tomato juice.

3 ▼ Place the cucumber and peppers in the food processor or blender and pulse on and off until finely chopped; do not overmix.

4 ▲ Reserve about 30ml/2 tbsp of the chopped vegetables for garnishing; stir the remainder into the soup base. Taste for seasoning. Mix in the chopped tomato, spring onions and a dash of hot pepper sauce, if you like. Chill well.

5 To serve, ladle into bowls and sprinkle with the reserved chopped vegetables, chopped fresh parsley or coriander, and croutons.

1 ▲ For the soup base, put the tomatoes in a food processor or blender and pulse on and off until just smooth, scraping the sides of the container occasionally.

Individual Goat's Cheese Tarts

SERVES 6

6–8 sheets filo pastry (about 115g/4oz)

50g/2oz/¼ cup butter, melted

350g/12oz firm log-shaped goat's cheese, rind removed

9 cherry tomatoes, quartered

120ml/4fl oz/½ cup milk

2 eggs

30ml/2 tbsp whipping cream

pinch of ground white pepper

mixed green salad, to serve (optional)

~ COOK'S TIP ~

Keep the filo pastry under a damp cloth while working to prevent the sheets from drying out.

1 Preheat oven to 190°C/375°F/Gas 5. Grease six 10cm/4in tart tins (pans).

2 ▲ For each tart, cut out four circles of filo pastry, each about 12cm/4½in in diameter. Place one circle in the tin and brush with some melted butter. Top with another filo circle and brush with butter. Continue until there are four layers of filo pastry; do not butter the last layer. Repeat the procedure for the remaining three tins.

3 ▲ Place the pastry-lined tins on a baking sheet. Cut the goat's cheese log into six slices. Place a slice in each of the pastry cases.

4 ▲ Arrange the tomato quarters around the cheese slices.

5 ▲ Combine the milk, eggs, cream and pepper in a measuring jug (cup) or bowl and whisk to mix. Pour into the pastry cases, filling them almost to the top.

6 Bake until puffed and golden, 30–40 minutes. Serve hot or warm, with a mixed green salad if you like.

Turkey and Avocado Pitta Bread Pizzas

SERVES 4

8 plum tomatoes, quartered
45–60ml/3–4 tbsp olive oil
salt and pepper
1 large ripe avocado
8 pitta bread rounds
6–7 slices of cooked turkey, chopped
1 onion, thinly sliced
275g/10oz/2½ cups grated Monterey Jack or Cheddar cheese
30ml/2 tbsp chopped fresh coriander (cilantro)

1 Preheat oven to 230°C/450°F/Gas 8.

2 ▲ Place the tomatoes in a baking dish. Drizzle over 15ml/1 tbsp of the olive oil and season with salt and pepper. Bake for 30 minutes; do not stir.

3 Remove the baking dish from the oven and mash the tomatoes with a fork, removing the skins as you mash. Set aside.

4 ▲ Peel and stone (pit) the avocado. Cut into 16 thin slices.

5 Brush the edges of the pitta breads with oil. Arrange the breads on two baking sheets.

6 ▼ Spread each pitta with mashed tomato, almost to the edges.

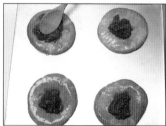

7 ▲ Top each with two avocado slices. Sprinkle with the turkey, then add a few onion slices. Season with salt and pepper. Sprinkle on the cheese.

8 Place one sheet in the middle of the oven and bake until the cheese begins to melt, 15–20 minutes. Sprinkle with half the coriander and serve. Meanwhile, bake the second batch of pizzas to serve them hot.

Crab Louis

SERVES 4

225g/8oz/4 cups Little Gem (Bibb) lettuce leaves

350g/12oz/2 cups fresh crab meat

4 hard-boiled eggs, sliced

4 tomatoes, quartered

½ green (bell) pepper, seeded and thinly sliced

50g/2oz/½ cup pitted black olives, sliced

FOR THE DRESSING

250ml/8fl oz/1 cup mayonnaise

10ml/2 tsp fresh lemon juice

50ml/2fl oz/¼ cup chilli sauce

½ green (bell) pepper, seeded and finely chopped

5ml/1 tsp prepared horseradish

5ml/1 tsp Worcestershire sauce

1 ▲ For the dressing, combine all the ingredients in a bowl and mix well. Set aside.

2 Line four salad plates with the lettuce leaves. Heap the crab meat in the centre. Arrange hard-boiled eggs and tomatoes around the outside.

3 ▼ Spoon some of the dressing over the crab. Arrange the green pepper slices on top and sprinkle with the olives. Serve at once, with the remaining dressing.

Poolside Tuna Salad

SERVES 4–6

175g/6oz radishes

1 cucumber

3 celery sticks

1 yellow (bell) pepper

175g/6oz cherry tomatoes, halved

4 spring onions (scallions), thinly sliced

2.5ml/½ tsp salt, or to taste

50ml/2fl oz/¼ cup fresh lemon juice

50ml/2fl oz/¼ cup olive oil

black pepper

2 x 200g/7oz cans tuna, drained

30ml/2 tbsp chopped fresh parsley

lettuce leaves, to serve

twisted lemon peel, to garnish

1 Cut the radishes, cucumber, celery and pepper into pea-size dice. Place in a large, shallow dish. Add the tomatoes and spring onions.

2 ▼ In a small bowl, stir together the salt and lemon juice with a fork until dissolved. Pour this over the vegetable mixture. Add the oil and pepper to taste. Stir to blend. Cover and leave to stand for 1 hour.

3 Add the tuna and parsley and toss gently until combined.

4 ▲ Arrange the lettuce leaves on a serving dish and heap the salad in the centre. Garnish with the lemon peel.

~ VARIATION ~

Prepare the vegetables as above and add the parsley. Arrange lettuce leaves on individual plates and divide the vegetable mixture between them. Place a mound of tuna on top of each and finish with a dollop of mayonnaise.

Crab Louis (top), Poolside Tuna Salad

Goat's Cheese Salad

<u>SERVES 4</u>

30ml/2 tbsp olive oil

4 slices of French bread, 1cm/½in thick

450g/1lb/8 cups mixed salad greens, such
   as curly endive, radicchio and
   red oak leaf, torn into small pieces

4 firm goat's cheese rounds, about
   50g/2oz each, rind removed

1 yellow or red (bell) pepper, seeded and
   finely diced

1 small red onion, thinly sliced

45ml/3 tbsp chopped fresh parsley

30ml/2 tbsp chopped fresh chives

FOR THE DRESSING

30ml/2 tbsp wine vinegar

1.5ml/¼ tsp salt

5ml/1 tsp wholegrain mustard

75ml/5 tbsp olive oil

black pepper

1 For the dressing, mix the vinegar
and salt with a fork until dissolved.
Stir in the mustard. Gradually stir in
the oil until blended. Season with
pepper and set aside.

2 Preheat the grill (broiler).

3 ▲ Heat the oil in a frying pan.
When hot, add the bread slices and
cook until golden, about 1 minute.
Turn and cook the other side, for about
30 seconds more. Drain on kitchen
paper and set aside.

4 ▲ Place the salad greens in a bowl.
Add 45ml/3 tbsp of the dressing and
toss to coat. Divide the dressed leaves
between four salad plates.

5 ▲ Put the goat's cheeses, cut side up,
on a baking sheet and grill (broil) until
bubbling and golden, 1–2 minutes.

6 Set one goat's cheese on each slice
of bread and place in the centre of
each plate. Scatter the diced pepper,
red onion, parsley and chives over
the salad. Drizzle with the remaining
dressing and serve.

~ **VARIATION** ~

For a more substantial main course
salad, increase the amount of
greens and make double the
quantity of dressing. Add 300g/11oz/
2 cups sliced cooked green beans and
300g/11oz/2 cups diced ham to the
greens, and toss with half the
dressing. Top with the grilled goat's
cheeses and remaining dressing.

Three-bean and Lentil Salad

SERVES 6

1 cup dried chickpeas, soaked overnight
  and drained

1 cup dried red kidney beans, soaked
  overnight and drained

3 bay leaves

30ml/2 tbsp sea salt

50g/2oz/½ cup lentils

225g/8oz fresh green beans, cut in
  2.5cm/1in slices and cooked

1 small red onion, finely chopped

3 spring onions (scallions), chopped

15ml/1 tbsp chopped fresh parsley

FOR THE DRESSING

75–90ml/5–6 tbsp red wine vinegar

5ml/1 tsp salt

10ml/2 tsp Dijon-style mustard

90ml/6 tbsp olive oil

1 garlic clove, finely chopped

black pepper

3 Halfway through the beans' cooking time, put the lentils in a large pan and add cold water to cover and the remaining bay leaf. Bring to the boil, then cover and simmer until just tender, 30–40 minutes.

4 ▼ As the lentils and the beans finish cooking, drain thoroughly in a colander and place them in a large bowl. Discard the bay leaves.

5 ▲ Add the green beans, red onion, spring onions and parsley to the bowl. Add the dressing and toss well.

6 Taste the salad and adjust the seasoning, adding more vinegar, salt and pepper if you want. Serve the salad at room temperature.

1 ▲ For the dressing, in a bowl mix 60ml/4 tbsp of the vinegar and the salt with a fork until dissolved. Stir in the mustard. Gradually stir in the oil until blended. Add the garlic and pepper to taste. Set aside.

2 Put the chickpeas and kidney beans in separate large pans. To each, add fresh cold water to cover and a bay leaf. Bring to the boil, then cover and simmer for 30 minutes. Add half the sea salt to each pan and continue simmering until tender, 30 minutes–1½ hours more.

Artichoke Pasta Salad

SERVES 4

105ml/7 tbsp olive oil

1 red (bell) pepper, quartered, seeded and thinly sliced

1 onion, halved and thinly sliced

5ml/1 tsp dried thyme

salt and pepper

45ml/3 tbsp sherry vinegar

450g/1lb pasta shapes, such as penne or fusilli

2 x 175g/6oz jars marinated artichoke hearts, drained and thinly sliced

150g/5oz cooked broccoli, chopped

20–25 salt-cured black olives, pitted and chopped

30ml/2 tbsp chopped fresh parsley

1 ▼ Heat 30ml/2 tbsp of the oil in a non-stick frying pan. Add the red pepper and onion and cook over a low heat until just soft, 8–10 minutes, stirring occasionally.

2 ▲ Stir in the thyme, 1.5ml/¼ tsp salt and the vinegar. Cook, stirring, for 30 seconds more, then set aside.

3 ▲ Bring a large pan of salted water to the boil. Add the pasta and cook until just tender (following the packet instructions for timing). Drain, rinse with hot water then drain again well. Transfer to a large bowl. Add 30ml/ 2 tbsp of the oil and toss well to coat.

4 ▲ Add the artichokes, broccoli, olives, parsley, onion mixture and remaining oil to the pasta. Season with salt and pepper. Stir to blend. Leave to stand for at least 1 hour before serving, or chill overnight. Serve at room temperature.

Asparagus with Creamy Raspberry Vinaigrette

SERVES 4

675g/1½lb thin asparagus spears

30ml/2 tbsp raspberry vinegar

2.5ml/½ tsp salt

5ml/1 tsp Dijon-style mustard

75ml/5 tbsp sunflower oil

30ml/2 tbsp sour cream or natural (plain) yogurt

white pepper

175g/6oz/1 cup raspberries, to garnish

1 Fill a large wide pan, frying pan or wok with water about 10cm/4in deep and bring to the boil.

2 ▲ Trim the tough ends of the asparagus spears. If you want, remove the "scales" using a vegetable peeler.

4 ▼ With a slotted fish slice or metal spatula, carefully remove the asparagus bundles from the boiling water and immerse in cold water to stop them cooking. Drain and untie the bundles. Pat dry with kitchen paper. Chill the asparagus for at least 1 hour.

5 ▲ Combine the vinegar and salt in a bowl and stir with a fork until dissolved. Stir in the mustard. Gradually stir in the oil until blended. Add the sour cream or yogurt and pepper to taste.

3 ▲ Tie the asparagus spears into two bundles. Lower into the boiling water and cook, keeping the bundles upright, until just tender, about 2 minutes.

6 To serve, place the asparagus on individual plates and drizzle the dressing across the middle of the spears. Garnish with the fresh raspberries and serve.

California Taco Salad with Beef

~ VARIATIONS ~

For California Taco Salad with Chicken, substitute 450g/1lb skinless chicken breast fillets, finely diced, for the minced beef. Chickpeas may be used in place of the kidney beans. Although frozen or canned corn is convenient, freshly cooked corn kernels scraped from the cob give added moisture and extra flavour.

1 ▲ For the dressing, mix the vinegar and salt with a fork until dissolved. Stir in the mustard and buttermilk. Gradually stir in the oil until blended. Add the garlic, cumin, oregano and pepper and set aside.

2 ▲ Heat the oil in a non-stick frying pan. Add the beef, onion, salt and cayenne and cook until just browned, 5–7 minutes. Stir frequently to break up the lumps. Drain and leave to cool.

3 ▲ In a large bowl, combine the beef, corn, kidney beans and chopped coriander and toss to blend.

4 ▲ Stack the lettuce leaves on top of one another and slice thinly, crossways, into shreds. Place in another bowl and toss with 50ml/2fl oz/¼ cup of the dressing. Divide the shredded lettuce between four dinner plates.

5 ▲ Heap the meat mixture in the centre of each plate. Arrange the tomatoes at the edge. Sprinkle with the grated cheese.

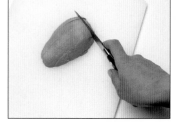

6 ▲ Peel, stone (pit) and dice the avocado. Scatter on top of the salad with the olives and spring onions.

7 Pour the remaining dressing over the salads. Garnish with coriander. Serve with tortilla chips.

Cheesy Courgette Casserole

SERVES 4

1 garlic clove, crushed with a knife

30ml/2 tbsp olive oil or melted butter

900g/2lb courgettes (zucchini)

salt and pepper

2 cups grated Monterey Jack or
    Cheddar cheese

2 eggs

350ml/12fl oz/1½ cups milk

~ VARIATIONS ~

For a spicier version, replace the
cheese with a chilli-flavoured cheese,
such as Jalapeño Jack, and toss the
courgettes in 10ml/2 tsp chilli powder.

---

1 Preheat oven to 190°C/375°F/Gas 5.

2 ▼ Rub the garlic clove around the
inside of a baking dish, pressing hard
to extract the juice; discard the garlic.
Grease the dish with half the oil or
melted butter.

3 ▲ Cut the courgettes across into
6mm/¼in slices. Place them in a bowl
and toss with the remaining oil or
melted butter and salt to taste.

4 ▲ Arrange half the courgette slices
in an even layer in the baking dish.
Sprinkle with half the cheese. Add
the remaining courgette slices,
spreading them evenly over the top.

5 ▲ Combine the eggs, milk,
2.5ml/½ tsp salt and pepper to taste in
a bowl and whisk together. Pour over
the courgettes. Sprinkle with the
remaining grated cheese.

6 Cover with foil and bake for about
30 minutes. Remove the foil and
continue baking until the top is
browned, 30–40 minutes more. Serve
hot, warm or cold.

San Francisco Chicken Wings

SERVES 4

75ml/2½fl oz/⅓ cup soy sauce
15ml/1 tbsp soft light brown sugar
15ml/1 tbsp rice vinegar
30ml/2 tbsp dry sherry
juice of 1 orange
5cm/2in strip of orange peel
1 star anise
5ml/1 tsp cornflour (cornstarch)
50ml/2fl oz/¼ cup water
15ml/1 tbsp finely chopped fresh root ginger
1.5–5ml/¼–1 tsp Oriental chilli-garlic sauce, to taste
1.6kg/3½lb chicken wings (22–24), tips removed

1 Preheat oven to 200°C/400°F/Gas 6.

2 ▲ Combine the soy sauce, brown sugar, vinegar, sherry, orange juice and peel and star anise in a pan. Bring to the boil over a medium heat.

3 ▲ Combine the cornflour and water in a small bowl and stir until blended. Add to the boiling soy sauce mixture, stirring well. Boil for 1 minute more, stirring constantly.

4 ▼ Remove the soy sauce mixture from the heat and stir in the finely chopped ginger and chilli-garlic sauce.

5 ▲ Arrange the chicken wings, in one layer, in a large baking dish. Pour over the soy sauce mixture and stir to coat the wings evenly.

6 Bake until tender and browned, 30–40 minutes, basting occasionally. Serve the wings hot or warm.

Swordfish with Pepper and Orange Relish

SERVES 4

75ml/5 tbsp olive oil

1 large fennel bulb, cut into 6mm/ ¼in dice

1 red (bell) pepper, seeded and cut into 6mm/¼in dice

1 yellow (bell) pepper, seeded and cut into 6mm/¼in dice

1 orange or green (bell) pepper, seeded and cut into 6mm/¼in dice

1 small onion, cut into 6mm/¼ in dice

5ml/1 tsp grated orange rind

50ml/2fl oz/¼ cup fresh orange juice

salt

4 pieces of swordfish steak, about 150g/5oz each

1 ▼ Heat 45ml/3 tbsp of the oil in a large non-stick frying pan. Add the fennel, peppers and onion and cook over a medium heat until just tender, about 5 minutes (they should retain some crunch).

2 ▲ Stir in the orange rind and juice and cook for 1 minute more. Stir in 2.5ml/½ tsp salt. Cover and set aside.

3 Bring some water to the boil in the bottom of a steamer.

4 ▲ Meanwhile, brush the fish steaks on both sides with the remaining oil and season with salt.

5 ▲ Place the fish steaks in the top part of the steamer. Cover the pan and steam until the steaks are opaque throughout, about 5 minutes.

6 Transfer the fish to dinner plates. Serve at once, accompanied by the pepper and orange relish.

Tangerine-Soy Marinated Salmon

SERVES 4

250ml/8fl oz/1 cup soy sauce

25ml/1½ tsp soft light brown sugar

50ml/2fl oz/¼ cup rice vinegar

15ml/1 tbsp finely chopped fresh
    root ginger

2 garlic cloves, finely chopped

grated rind and juice of 1 tangerine

120ml/4fl oz/½ cup water

4 pieces of salmon fillet, about
    175g/6oz each

3 Preheat oven to 180°C/350°F/Gas 4.

4 ▼ Remove the fish from the
marinade, leaving on any pieces of
ginger that cling to the fish. Place in a
baking dish, in one layer.

5 ▲ Cover the dish with foil. Bake
until the fish is opaque throughout,
20–30 minutes. Transfer to four dinner
plates and serve at once. This dish is
good served with steamed broccoli.

1 ▲ Combine the soy sauce, sugar,
vinegar, ginger, garlic, orange rind
and juice and water in a bowl. Stir
until well blended.

2 ▲ Arrange the fish, in one layer, in
a large shallow dish. Pour over the soy
sauce mixture and turn the fish so that
both sides are coated. Cover and leave
to marinate at room temperature for
1 hour, or chill overnight.

Cioppino

SERVES 4

300ml/2 tbsp olive oil

1 onion, halved and thinly sliced

several saffron threads, crushed

5ml/1 tsp dried thyme

pinch of cayenne pepper

salt and pepper

2 garlic cloves, finely chopped

2 x 400g/14oz cans peeled tomatoes,
   drained and chopped

175ml/6fl oz/¾ cup dry white wine

2.5 litres/4 pints fish stock

350g/12oz skinless fish fillets,
   cut into pieces

450g/1lb monkfish, membrane removed,
   cut into pieces

450g/1lb mussels in shell,
   thoroughly scrubbed

225g/8oz small squid bodies, cleaned
   and cut into rings

30ml/2 tbsp chopped fresh parsley

thickly sliced sourdough bread,
   to serve

1 ▼ Heat the oil in a large, heavy pan. Add the onion, saffron, thyme, cayenne and 2.5ml/½ tsp salt. Stir well and cook over a low heat until soft, 8–10 minutes. Add the garlic and cook for 1 minute more.

~ COOK'S TIP ~

Do not prepare mussels more than a few hours in advance of cooking or they will spoil and die.

2 ▲ Stir in the tomatoes, wine and fish stock. Bring to the boil and boil for 1 minute, then reduce the heat to medium-low and simmer for 15 minutes.

3 ▲ Add the fish fillet and monkfish pieces to the pan and simmer gently for 3 minutes.

4 ▲ Add the mussels and squid and simmer until the mussel shells open, about 2 minutes more. Stir in the parsley. Season with salt and pepper.

5 Ladle into warmed soup bowls and serve at once, with bread.

Prawn Kebabs with Plum Sauce

SERVES 6

15ml/1 tbsp vegetable oil

1 onion, finely chopped

1 garlic clove, finely chopped

450g/1lb purple plums, stoned (pitted) and chopped

15ml/1 tbsp rice vinegar

30ml/2 tbsp fresh orange juice

5ml/1 tsp Dijon-style mustard

30ml/2 tbsp soy sauce

15ml/1 tbsp soft light brown sugar

1 point of a star anise

120ml/4fl oz/½ cup water

675g/1½lb medium-size raw prawns, peeled (tails left on if desired) and deveined

boiled rice, to serve

1 ▲ Heat the oil in a pan. Add the onion, garlic and plums and cook over a low heat, stirring occasionally, until softened, about 10 minutes.

2 Stir in the vinegar, orange juice, mustard, soy sauce, sugar, star anise and water. Bring to the boil. Lower the heat, cover and simmer, stirring occasionally, for 20 minutes.

3 Uncover the pan and simmer the sauce for 10 minutes more to thicken, stirring frequently.

4 ▼ Remove the star anise. Transfer to a food processor or blender and purée until smooth.

5 Press the sauce through a fine strainer to remove all the fibres and plum skins.

6 Preheat the grill (broiler).

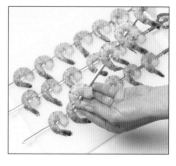

7 ▲ Thread the prawns, flat, on to six skewers. Brush them all over with three-quarters of the plum sauce.

8 Place the prawn kebabs on a foil-lined grill (broiling) pan. Grill (broil) until opaque throughout, 5–6 minutes. Turn the kebabs once.

9 Meanwhile, reheat the remaining plum sauce. Serve the kebabs with rice and the sauce.

Lemon Chicken with Guacamole Sauce

SERVES 4

juice of 2 lemons

45ml/3 tbsp olive oil

2 garlic cloves, finely chopped

salt and pepper

4 chicken breasts, about 200g/7oz each

2 beefsteak tomatoes, cored and
  cut in half

chopped fresh coriander (cilantro),
  to garnish

FOR THE SAUCE

1 ripe avocado

50ml/2fl oz/¼ cup sour cream

45ml/3 tbsp fresh lemon juice

2.5ml/½ tsp salt

50ml/2fl oz/¼ cup water

2 ▲ Arrange the chicken breasts, in one layer, in a shallow glass or ceramic dish. Pour over the lemon mixture and turn to coat evenly. Cover and leave to stand for at least 1 hour at room temperature, or chill overnight.

3 ▲ For the sauce, cut the avocado in half, remove the stone (pit) and scrape the flesh into a food processor or blender.

1 ▲ Combine the lemon juice, oil, garlic, 2.5ml/½ tsp salt and a little pepper in a bowl. Stir to mix.

~ VARIATION ~

To grill the chicken, prepare the fire, and when the coals are glowing red and covered with grey ash, spread them in a single layer. Set an oiled grill rack about 13cm/5in above the coals and cook the chicken breasts until lightly charred and cooked through, about 15–20 minutes. Allow extra olive oil for basting.

4 ▲ Add the sour cream, lemon juice and salt and process until smooth. Add the water and process just to blend. If necessary, add more water to thin the sauce. Transfer to a bowl, taste and adjust the seasoning, if necessary. Set aside.

5 ▲ Preheat the grill (broiler). Heat a ridged frying pan. Remove the chicken from the marinade and pat dry.

6 ▲ When the frying pan is hot, add the chicken breasts and cook, turning often, until they are cooked through, about 10 minutes.

7 ▲ Meanwhile, arrange the tomato halves, cut-sides up, on a baking sheet and season lightly with salt and pepper. Grill (broil) until hot and bubbling, about 5 minutes.

8 To serve, place a chicken breast, tomato half and a dollop of avocado sauce on each plate. Sprinkle with coriander and serve.

Poussins with Raisin and Walnut Stuffing

SERVES 4

250ml/8fl oz/1 cup port
100g/3¾oz/⅔ cup raisins
15ml/1 tbsp walnut oil
75g/3oz mushrooms, finely chopped
1 large celery stick, finely chopped
1 small onion, chopped
salt and pepper
50g/2oz/1 cup fresh breadcrumbs
50g/2oz/½ cup chopped walnuts
15ml/1 tbsp each chopped fresh basil and parsley, or 30ml/2 tbsp chopped parsley
2.5ml/½ tsp dried thyme
75g/3oz/6 tbsp butter, melted
4 poussins

1 Preheat oven to 180°C/350°F/Gas 4.

2 In a small bowl, combine the port and raisins and leave to soak for about 20 minutes.

3 ▲ Meanwhile, heat the oil in a non-stick frying pan. Add the mushrooms, celery, onion and 1.5ml/¼ tsp salt and cook over a low heat until softened, 8–10 minutes. Leave to cool slightly.

4 ▲ Drain the raisins, reserving the port. Combine the raisins, breadcrumbs, walnuts, basil, parsley and thyme in a bowl. Stir in the onion mixture and 60ml/4 tbsp of the melted butter. Add 2.5ml/½ tsp salt and pepper to taste.

5 ▲ Fill the cavity of each poussin with the stuffing mixture, but do not pack it down. Tie the legs together, looping the tail with the string to enclose the stuffing securely.

6 Brush the poussins with the remaining butter and place in a baking dish that is just large enough to hold the birds comfortably. Pour over the reserved port.

7 Roast, basting occasionally, for about 1 hour. To test if the birds are done, pierce the thigh with a skewer; the juices should run clear. Serve at once, pouring some of the pan juices over each bird.

Fusilli with Turkey, Tomatoes and Broccoli

SERVES 4

675g/1½lb ripe but firm plum
   tomatoes, quartered

90ml/6 tbsp olive oil

5ml/1 tsp dried oregano

salt and pepper

350g/12oz broccoli florets

1 small onion, sliced

5ml/1 tsp dried thyme

450g/1lb skinless boneless
   turkey breast, cubed

3 garlic cloves, finely chopped

15ml/1 tbsp fresh lemon juice

450g/1lb fusilli

1 Preheat oven to 200°C/400°F/Gas 6.

2 ▲ Place the tomatoes in a baking
dish. Add 15ml/1 tbsp of the oil, the
oregano and 2.5ml/½ tsp salt and stir
to blend.

3 Bake until the tomatoes are just
browned, 30–40 minutes; do not stir.

4 Meanwhile, bring a large pan of
salted water to the boil. Add the
broccoli and cook until just tender,
about 5 minutes. Drain and set aside.
(Alternatively, steam the broccoli
until tender.)

5 ▲ Heat 30ml/2 tbsp of the oil in
a large non-stick frying pan. Add the
onion, thyme, cubes of turkey and
2.5ml/½ tsp salt. Cook over a high
heat, stirring often, until the meat is
cooked and beginning to brown,
5–7 minutes. Add the garlic and cook
for 1 minute more, stirring frequently.

6 Remove from the heat. Stir in the
lemon juice and season with pepper.
Set aside and keep warm.

7 Bring another large pan of salted
water to the boil. Add the fusilli and
cook until just tender (follow the
packet instructions for timing). Drain
and place in a large bowl. Toss with
the remaining oil.

8 ▼ Add the broccoli to the turkey
mixture. Add to the fusilli. Add the
tomatoes and stir gently to blend.
Serve at once.

Chicken with White Wine, Olives and Garlic

SERVES 4

1.6kg/3½lb chicken,
    cut into serving pieces

1 onion, sliced

salt and pepper

3–6 garlic cloves, to taste, finely chopped

5ml/1 tsp dried thyme

475ml/16fl oz/2 cups dry white wine

175g/6oz/1 cup green olives
    (16–18), pitted

1 bay leaf

15ml/1 tbsp lemon juice

15–25g/½–1oz/1–2 tbsp butter

1 Heat a deep, heavy cast iron frying pan. When hot, add the chicken pieces, skin side down, and cook over a medium heat until browned, about 10 minutes. Turn and brown the other side, 5–8 minutes more. (Work in batches if necessary.)

2 Transfer the chicken pieces to a serving dish and set aside.

3 Drain the excess fat from the frying pan, leaving about 15ml/1 tbsp. Add the onion and 2.5ml/½ tsp salt and cook until just soft, about 5 minutes. Add the garlic and thyme and cook for 1 minute more.

4 ▼ Add the wine and stir, scraping up any bits that cling to the pan. Bring to the boil and boil for 1 minute. Stir in the green olives.

5 ▲ Return the chicken pieces to the pan. Add the bay leaf and season lightly with pepper. Lower the heat, cover and simmer until the chicken is cooked through, 20–30 minutes.

6 Transfer the chicken pieces to a warmed serving dish. Stir the lemon juice into the sauce. Whisk in the butter to thicken the sauce slightly. Spoon over the chicken and serve at once.

Turkey Meat Loaf

SERVES 4

15ml/1 tbsp olive oil

1 onion, chopped

1 green (bell) pepper, seeded and
    finely chopped

1 garlic clove, finely chopped

450g/1lb turkey mince

50g/2oz/1 cup fresh breadcrumbs

1 egg, beaten

75g/3oz/½ cup pine nuts

12 sun-dried tomatoes in oil, drained
    and chopped

75ml/2½fl oz/⅓ cup milk

10ml/2 tsp chopped fresh rosemary, or
    2.5ml/½ tsp dried rosemary

5ml/1 tsp ground fennel

2.5ml/½ tsp dried oregano

2.5ml/½ tsp salt

1 Preheat oven to 190°C/375°F/Gas 5.

2 ▼ Heat the oil in a frying pan. Add the onion, pepper and garlic and cook over a low heat, stirring often, until just softened, 8–10 minutes. Remove from the heat and leave to cool.

3 Place the turkey in a large bowl. Add the onion mixture and the remaining ingredients and mix thoroughly together.

4 ▲ Transfer to a 21 × 12cm/8½ × 4½in loaf tin (pan), packing the mixture down firmly. Bake until golden brown, about 1 hour. Serve hot or cold.

Chicken with White Wine, Olives and Garlic (top), Turkey Meat Loaf

Pork Chops with Chilli and Nectarine Relish

250ml/8fl oz/1 cup fresh orange juice

45ml/3 tbsp olive oil

2 garlic cloves, finely chopped

5ml/1 tsp ground cumin

15ml/1 tbsp coarsely ground
   black pepper

8 pork loin chops, about 2cm/¾in thick,
   well trimmed

salt

FOR THE RELISH

1 small fresh green chilli

30ml/2 tbsp honey

juice of ½ lemon

250ml/8fl oz/1 cup chicken stock

2 nectarines, stoned (pitted) and chopped

1 garlic clove, finely chopped

½ onion, finely chopped

5ml/1 tsp finely chopped fresh root ginger

1.5ml/¼ tsp salt

15ml/1 tbsp chopped fresh
   coriander (cilantro)

1 For the relish, roast the chilli over a gas flame, holding it with tongs, until charred on all sides. (Alternatively, char the skin under the grill/broiler.) Leave to cool for 5 minutes.

2 ▼ Wearing rubber gloves, carefully remove the charred skin of the chilli. Discard the seeds if a less hot flavour is desired. Finely chop the chilli and place in a heavy pan.

3 ▲ Add the honey, lemon juice, chicken stock, nectarines, garlic, onion, ginger and salt. Bring to a boil, then simmer, stirring occasionally, for about 30 minutes. Stir in the coriander and set aside.

4 In a small bowl, combine the orange juice, oil, garlic, cumin and pepper. Stir to mix.

5 ▲ Arrange the pork chops, in one layer, in a shallow dish. Pour over the orange juice mixture and turn to coat. Cover and leave to stand for at least 1 hour, or chill overnight.

6 Remove the pork from the marinade and pat dry with kitchen paper. Season lightly with salt.

7 Heat a ridged frying pan. When hot, add the pork chops and cook until browned, about 5 minutes. Turn and cook on the other side until done, about 10 minutes more. (Work in batches if necessary.) Serve at once, with the relish.

Roast Leg of Lamb with Pesto

SERVES 6

115g/4oz/2 cups fresh basil leaves

4 garlic cloves, coarsely chopped

45ml/3 tbsp pine nuts

150ml/¼ pint/⅔ cup olive oil

50g/2oz/⅔ cup freshly grated
Parmesan cheese

5ml/1 tsp salt, or to taste

2.25–2.75kg/5–6lb leg of lamb

5 ▲ Continue patting on the pesto in a thick, even layer. Cover and leave to stand for 2 hours at room temperature, or chill overnight.

6 Preheat the oven to 180°C/350°F/Gas 4.

7 Place the lamb in the oven and roast, allowing about 20 minutes per 450g/1lb for rare meat and 25 minutes for medium-rare. Turn the lamb occasionally during roasting.

8 Remove the leg of lamb from the oven, cover it loosely with foil and leave it to rest for about 15 minutes before carving and serving.

1 ▲ To make the pesto, combine the basil, garlic and pine nuts in a food processor, and process until finely chopped. With the motor running, slowly add the oil in a steady stream.

2 Scrape the mixture into a bowl. Stir in the Parmesan and salt.

3 ▲ Place the lamb in a roasting dish. Make several slits in the meat with a sharp knife and spoon some pesto into each slit.

4 Rub more pesto over the surface of the lamb.

Beef and Aubergine Stir-fry with Ginger

SERVES 4–6

600g/1lb 6oz boneless beef, such as flank steak, thinly sliced

30ml/2 tbsp soy sauce, plus extra for serving

450g/1lb aubergine (eggplant)

45ml/3 tbsp water

30ml/2 tbsp rice vinegar

15ml/1 tbsp dry sherry

5ml/1 tsp honey

5ml/1 tsp red pepper flakes

50ml/2fl oz/¼ cup vegetable oil

15ml/1 tbsp sesame oil

1 garlic clove, finely chopped

15ml/1 tbsp finely chopped fresh root ginger

boiled rice, to serve

1 ▲ Combine the beef and soy sauce in a shallow dish. Stir to coat evenly. Cover and leave to marinate for 1 hour, or chill overnight.

~ VARIATIONS ~

For Turkey and Aubergine Stir-fry, substitute thinly sliced turkey breast for the beef. If time is short, it is not essential to precook the aubergine, but microwaving or steaming the aubergine before stir-frying helps to eliminate any bitterness and also prevents the aubergine from soaking up too much oil.

2 ▲ Cut the aubergine into eighths lengthways. Trim away the inner part with the seeds, leaving a flat edge. Cut the aubergine slices on the diagonal into diamond shapes that are about 2.5cm/1in wide.

3 ▲ Place the aubergine in a large microwaveable dish. Stir in the water. Cover and microwave on high (650 watt) for 3 minutes. Stir gently, then microwave for 3 minutes more. Set aside, still covered. (Alternatively, steam the aubergine over boiling water until tender, if preferred.)

4 ▲ In a small bowl, combine the vinegar, sherry, honey and red pepper flakes. Stir to mix. Set aside.

5 ▲ Heat 15ml/1 tbsp vegetable oil and 5ml/1 tsp sesame oil in a large non-stick frying pan or wok. Add half the beef, garlic and ginger. Cook over a high heat, stirring frequently, until the beef is just cooked through, 2–3 minutes. Remove to a bowl. Cook the remaining beef, garlic and ginger in the same way. Add to the bowl and set aside.

6 ▲ Heat the remaining vegetable and sesame oils in the frying pan or wok. Add the aubergine and cook over moderate heat until just browned and tender, about 5 minutes. (Work in two batches if necessary.)

7 Return the beef to the frying pan or wok. Stir in the vinegar mixture and cook just until the liquid is absorbed, 2–3 minutes more. Taste for seasoning. Serve at once, with rice and extra soy sauce.

Berry Salsa

MAKES 675G/1½LB/3 CUPS

1 fresh jalapeño pepper
½ red onion, finely chopped
2 spring onions (scallions), chopped
1 tomato, finely diced
1 small yellow (bell) pepper, seeded and finely chopped
15g/½oz/¼ cup chopped fresh coriander (cilantro)
1.5ml/¼ tsp salt
15ml/1 tbsp raspberry vinegar
15ml/1 tbsp fresh orange juice
5ml/1 tsp honey
15ml/1 tbsp olive oil
300ml/½ pint strawberries, hulled
300ml/½ pint blueberries or blackberries
300ml/½ pint raspberries

1 ▼ Wearing rubber gloves, finely chop the jalapeño pepper (discarding the seeds and membrane if a less hot flavour is desired). Place the pepper in a medium bowl.

2 ▲ Add the red onion, spring onions, tomato, pepper and coriander and stir to blend.

3 ▲ In a small measuring jug (cup), whisk together the salt, vinegar, orange juice, honey and oil. Pour over the jalapeño mixture and stir well.

4 ▲ Coarsely chop the strawberries. Add to the jalapeño mixture with the other berries and stir to blend. Leave to stand at room temperature for 3 hours.

5 Serve the salsa at room temperature, with grilled fish or poultry.

Fresh Pineapple and Mint Chutney

MAKES 675G/1½LB/3 CUPS

250ml/8fl oz/1 cup raspberry vinegar
250ml/8fl oz/1 cup dry white wine
1 small pineapple, skin removed and flesh chopped
2 medium oranges, peeled and chopped
1 apple, peeled and chopped
1 red (bell) pepper, seeded and diced
1½ onions, finely chopped
50g/2oz/¼ cup honey
pinch of salt
1 clove
4 black peppercorns
30ml/2 tbsp chopped fresh mint

1 ▲ In a pan, combine the vinegar and wine and bring to the boil. Boil for 3 minutes.

2 ▲ Add the remaining ingredients, except the mint, and stir to blend. Simmer gently for about 30 minutes, stirring occasionally.

3 Transfer to a strainer set over a bowl and drain, pressing down to extract the liquid. Remove and discard the clove and peppercorns. Set the fruit mixture aside.

4 ▼ Return the strained juice to the pan and boil until reduced by two-thirds. Pour over the fruit mixture.

5 ▲ Stir in the mint. Leave the chutney to stand for 6–8 hours before serving, with pork or lamb dishes.

~ COOK'S TIP ~

The chutney will keep about 1 week in the refrigerator.

Aubergine Ratatouille

SERVES 6

1.6kg/3½lb aubergines (about 4)

45ml/3 tbsp olive oil

1 large onion, sliced

salt and pepper

3 garlic cloves, finely chopped

2 x 400g/14oz cans peeled plum tomatoes, drained and chopped

30ml/2 tbsp chopped fresh basil, or 5ml/1 tsp dried basil

fresh basil leaves, for garnishing

1 Cut the aubergines into large cubes. Bring a large pan of salted water to the boil. Add the aubergine and cook for 3–4 minutes. Drain thoroughly.

2 ▼ Heat 30ml/2 tbsp of the oil in a large frying pan. Add the onion and 1.5ml/¼ tsp salt and cook over a low heat until just soft, 8–10 minutes.

3 Add the garlic, aubergine and remaining oil and stir to mix. Cook gently for about 5 minutes.

4 ▲ Stir in the tomatoes and basil. Season with salt and pepper. Cover and cook over a low heat until the aubergine is very tender, about 30 minutes, stirring occasionally.

5 Sprinkle the ratatouille with fresh basil leaves and serve.

Garlicky Sautéed Courgettes

SERVES 4

6 medium courgettes (zucchini)

30ml/2 tbsp olive oil

2.5ml/½ tsp salt

4–6 garlic cloves, finely chopped

5ml/1 tsp dried thyme

15ml/1 tbsp fresh lemon juice

black pepper

~ VARIATION ~

For Pasta with Courgette Sauce, add 2 x 400g/14oz cans peeled plum tomatoes, roughly chopped, to the browned courgettes instead of the lemon juice. Simmer until thickened, 5–10 minutes longer. Serve with boiled pasta shapes and sprinkle with grated Parmesan cheese, if you like.

1 ▼ Trim the ends of the courgettes, then halve and quarter them lengthways. Cut into slices about 2cm/¾in thick.

2 Heat the oil in a large non-stick frying pan. Add the courgette and toss to coat evenly. Add the salt and stir, then leave to cook until browned on one side, about 5 minutes.

3 ▲ Add the garlic and thyme. Shake the pan and turn the courgette with the aid of a wooden spatula. Continue cooking until golden brown on both sides and tender, about 5 minutes more. Do not let the garlic burn; if necessary, reduce the heat and increase the cooking time slightly.

4 Stir in the lemon juice, season liberally with black pepper and serve.

Aubergine Ratatouille (top), Garlicky Sautéed Courgettes

Herbed Goat's Cheese Dip

MAKES ABOUT 450G/1LB/2 CUPS

275g/10oz soft mild goat's cheese

120ml/4fl oz/½ cup single (light) or pouring (half-and-half) cream

10ml/2 tsp fresh lemon juice

15ml/1 tbsp chopped fresh chives

15ml/1 tbsp chopped fresh parsley

30ml/2 tbsp chopped fresh basil

black pepper

raw or briefly cooked cold vegetables, crisps (US potato chips) or savoury biscuits (crackers), to serve

1 ▼ In a food processor or blender, combine the goat's cheese and cream and process to blend. Add the lemon juice and process until smooth.

2 ▲ Scrape into a bowl. Stir in the chives, parsley, basil and pepper to taste. Serve cold, as a dip for vegetables, crisps or savoury biscuits.

Avocado Dressing

MAKES ABOUT 350ML/12FL OZ/1½ CUPS

30ml/2 tbsp wine vinegar

2.5ml/½ tsp salt, or to taste

2.5ml/¾ tsp white pepper

½ red onion, coarsely chopped

45ml/3 tbsp olive oil

1 large ripe avocado, halved and stone (pit) removed

15ml/1 tbsp fresh lemon juice

45ml/3 tbsp natural (plain) yogurt

45ml/3 tbsp water, or as needed

30ml/2 tbsp chopped fresh coriander (cilantro)

raw or briefly cooked cold vegetables, for serving

1 ▲ In a bowl, combine the vinegar and salt and stir with a fork to dissolve. Stir in the pepper, chopped red onion and olive oil.

3 ▲ Add the yogurt and water and process until smooth. If you like, add more water to thin. Taste and adjust the seasoning if necessary.

~ COOK'S TIP ~

This versatile dressing need not be limited to serving with salads and crudités. Serve it as a sauce with grilled chicken or fish, or use it on sandwiches in place of mayonnaise or mustard, or to provide a cool contrast to any sort of spicy food.

2 ▲ Scoop the avocado flesh into a food processor or blender. Add the lemon juice and onion dressing and process just to blend.

4 ▲ Scrape into a bowl. Stir in the coriander. Serve at once, as a dressing for salads, or use as a dip for raw or briefly cooked cold vegetables.

Herbed Goat's Cheese Dip (top), Avocado Dressing

Zinfandel Poached Pears

SERVES 4

1 bottle of red Zinfandel wine

150g/5oz/¾ cup granulated sugar

45ml/3 tbsp honey

juice of ½ lemon

1 cinnamon stick

1 vanilla pod (bean),
   split open lengthways

5cm/2in piece of orange peel

1 clove

1 black peppercorn

4 firm, ripe pears

whipped cream or sour cream,
   to serve

1 ▼ In a pan just large enough to hold the pears standing upright, combine the wine, sugar, honey, lemon juice, cinnamon, vanilla pod, orange peel, clove and peppercorn. Heat gently, stirring occasionally, until the sugar has dissolved.

2 ▲ Meanwhile, peel the pears, leaving the core and stem intact. Slice a small piece off the base of each pear so it will stand upright.

3 ▲ Gently place the pears in the wine mixture. Simmer, uncovered, until the pears are just tender, about 20–35 minutes depending on size and ripeness; do not overcook.

4 ▲ With a slotted spoon, gently transfer the pears to a bowl. Continue to boil the poaching liquid until reduced by about half. Leave to cool.

5 Strain the cooled liquid over the pears and chill for at least 3 hours.

6 Place the pears in serving dishes and spoon over the liquid. Serve with whipped cream or sour cream.

Baked Peaches with Raspberry Sauce

SERVES 6

40g/1½oz/3 tbsp unsalted butter,
    at room temperature

50g/2oz/¼ cup granulated sugar

1 egg, beaten

50g/2oz/½ cup ground almonds

6 ripe peaches

FOR THE SAUCE

175g/6oz/1 cup raspberries

15ml/1 tbsp icing (confectioners') sugar

15ml/1 tbsp fruit-flavoured
    brandy (optional)

1 Preheat the oven to 180°C/350°F/
Gas 4.

2 ▲ Beat the butter with the sugar
until soft and fluffy. Beat in the egg.
Add the ground almonds and beat just
to blend well together.

3 ▲ Halve the peaches and remove
the stones (pits). With a spoon, scrape
out some of the flesh from each peach
half, slightly enlarging the hollow left
by the stone. Reserve the excess peach
flesh to use in the sauce.

4 ▼ Place the peach halves on a
baking sheet (if necessary, secure with
crumpled foil to keep them steady).
Fill the hollow in each peach half with
the almond mixture.

5 Bake until the almond filling is
puffed and golden and the peaches are
very tender, about 30 minutes.

6 ▲ Meanwhile, for the sauce,
combine all the ingredients in a food
processor or blender. Add the reserved
peach flesh. Process until smooth.
Press through a strainer set over a
bowl to remove fibres and seeds.

7 Let the peaches cool slightly. Place
two peach halves on each plate and
spoon over some of the sauce. Serve
at once.

Chocolate, Coconut and Macadamia Parfait

◊SERVES 10

250g/8oz white chocolate, chopped

600ml/1 pint/2½ cups whipping cream

120ml/4fl oz/½ cup milk

10 egg yolks

15ml/1 tbsp granulated sugar

40g/1½oz/½ cup desiccated (dry unsweetened shredded) coconut, plus more to garnish

120ml/4fl oz/½ cup canned sweetened coconut cream

150g/5oz unsalted macadamia nuts

FOR THE GLAZE

225g/8oz dark (bittersweet) chocolate

75g/3oz/6 tbsp butter

20ml/4 tsp golden (light corn) syrup

175ml/6fl oz/¾ cup whipping cream

1 ▲ Line the bottom and sides of a 25 × 10cm/10 × 4in terrine dish with clear film (plastic wrap).

2 ▲ Combine the white chocolate and 50ml/2fl oz/¼ cup of the cream in the top of a double boiler or in a heat-proof bowl set over hot water. Stir until melted and smooth. Set aside.

3 Put 250ml/8fl oz/1 cup of the cream and the milk in a heavy pan and scald over a medium heat.

4 ▲ Meanwhile, in a large bowl, beat the egg yolks and sugar together until thick and pale.

5 ▲ Add the hot cream mixture to the yolks, beating constantly. Pour back into the pan and cook over a low heat until thickened, 2–3 minutes. Stir constantly and do not boil. Remove from the heat.

6 Stir in the melted chocolate, desiccated coconut and coconut cream until blended. Leave to cool.

7 Whip the remaining cream until thick. Fold into the chocolate and coconut mixture.

8 Put 475ml/16fl oz/2 cups of the parfait mixture in the prepared dish and spread evenly. Cover and freeze until just firm, about 2 hours. Cover the remaining mixture and chill.

9 ▲ Arrange the macadamia nuts evenly over the frozen parfait layer. Pour in the remaining parfait mixture. Cover the dish and freeze until the parfait is firm, 6–8 hours or overnight.

10 ▲ For the glaze, combine the dark chocolate, butter, and golden syrup in the top of a double boiler and stir occasionally until melted.

11 In a pan, heat the cream until just simmering. Stir into the chocolate mixture. Remove from the heat and leave to cool to lukewarm.

12 To turn out the parfait, wrap the dish in a hot towel and set it upside down on a plate. Peel off the clear film. Set the parfait on a rack over a baking sheet. Pour the glaze evenly over the top. Working quickly, smooth the glaze down the sides with a palette knife. Leave to set slightly, then sprinkle with desiccated coconut. Freeze for about 3–4 hours more.

13 To serve the parfait, slice it with a knife dipped in hot water.

Lemon Pound Cake

SERVES 8–10

275g/10oz/1¼ cups unsalted butter, at room temperature

375g/13oz/1¾ cups granulated sugar

6 eggs

grated rind and juice of 1 large lemon

265g/9½oz/2⅓ cups sifted self-raising (self-rising) flour

2.5ml/½ tsp salt

icing (confectioners') sugar, for dusting

1 Preheat the oven to 180°C/350°F/ Gas 4. Grease a 2.25 litre/3¾ pint/9 cup bundt tin (pan).

2 Beat the butter until it is soft and creamy. Gradually add the sugar and continue beating until fluffy.

3 ▼ Beat in the eggs, one at a time, beating well after each addition. Beat in the lemon rind and juice. Fold in the flour and salt in three batches.

4 Pour the mixture into the prepared tin and smooth the surface.

5 ▲ Bake until a skewer inserted in the centre comes out clean, 40–50 minutes. Leave to cool for 10 minutes before turning out on to a wire rack.

6 When the cake is cold, dust it with icing sugar.

Piña Colada Fruit Salad

SERVES 4

1 large pineapple

2 kiwi fruit

15g/½oz/¼ cup slivered fresh coconut

30ml/2 tbsp fresh lime juice

5ml/1 tsp granulated sugar

15–30ml/1–2 tbsp rum

8 large strawberries, halved

1 ▲ Cut a thick slice off one long side of the pineapple, not cutting into the crown of leaves.

2 ▼ Using a sharp spoon or a grapefruit knife, scoop out the flesh, taking care not to puncture the skin. Cut out and discard the core. Set the pineapple boat aside.

3 Chop the scooped-out flesh into bitesize pieces, keeping any juice, and place in a bowl.

4 Peel the kiwi fruit and chop into bitesize pieces. Add the kiwi fruit and coconut to the pineapple pieces.

5 ▲ In a small bowl, combine the lime juice, sugar and rum to taste. Stir to blend, then pour over the fruit. Toss well. Cover and chill the fruit salad for 1 hour.

6 To serve, spoon the fruit mixture into the pineapple boat. Garnish with the strawberries and serve at once.

Lemon Pound Cake (top), Piña Colada Fruit Salad

THE NORTHWEST

AN AREA THAT ENCOMPASSES SOME OF THE MOST MODERN CITIES AND WILDEST TERRAIN ALSO PROVIDES CULINARY CONTRASTS. MUCH OF IT OFFERS GOOD HUNTING AND FISHING TERRITORY, WHICH ARE COMPLEMENTED BY ORCHARDS AND AGRICULTURAL CULTIVATION, AS WELL AS ARTISANAL WINE AND CHEESEMAKING.

Salmon Chowder

SERVES 4

20g/¾ oz/1½ tbsp butter or margarine

1 onion, finely chopped

1 leek, finely chopped

50g/2oz/½ cup finely chopped
    fennel bulb

25g/1oz/¼ cup plain (all-purpose) flour

1.75 litres/3 pints fish stock

2 potatoes, cut into 1cm/½in cubes

salt and pepper

450g/1lb skinless salmon fillet,
    cut into 2cm/¾in cubes

175ml/6fl oz/¾ cup milk

120ml/4fl oz/½ cup whipping cream

30ml/2 tbsp chopped fresh dill

1 ▲ Melt the butter or margarine in a large pan. Add the onion, leek and fennel and cook over a medium heat until softened, 5–8 minutes, stirring the vegetables occasionally.

2 Stir in the flour. Reduce the heat to low and cook, stirring occasionally, for 3 minutes.

3 ▲ Add the stock and potatoes. Season with salt and pepper. Bring to the boil, then reduce the heat, cover and simmer until the potatoes are tender, about 20 minutes.

4 ▲ Add the salmon and simmer until just cooked, 3–5 minutes.

5 ▲ Stir in the milk, cream and dill. Cook just until warmed through; do not boil. Taste and adjust the seasoning, if necessary, then serve.

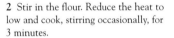

Smoked Turkey and Lentil Soup

SERVES 4

25g/1oz/2 tbsp butter
1 large carrot, chopped
1 onion, chopped
1 celery stick, chopped
1 leek, white part only, chopped
115g/4oz mushrooms, chopped
50ml/2fl oz/¼ cup dry white wine
1 litre/1¾ pints/4 cups chicken stock
10ml/2 tsp dried thyme
1 bay leaf
115g/4oz/½ cup lentils
225g/8oz smoked turkey meat, diced
salt and pepper
chopped fresh parsley, to garnish

1 ▲ Melt the butter in a large pan. Add the carrot, onion, leek, celery and mushrooms. Cook until golden, 3–5 minutes.

2 ▲ Stir in the wine and chicken stock. Bring to the boil and skim any foam that rises to the surface. Add the thyme and bay leaf. Lower the heat, cover and simmer gently for 30 minutes.

3 ▼ Add the lentils and continue cooking, covered, until they are just tender, 30–40 minutes more. Stir the soup from time to time.

4 ▲ Stir in the turkey and season to taste with salt and pepper. Cook until just heated through. Ladle into bowls and garnish with parsley.

Tomato and Blue Cheese Soup with Bacon

SERVES 4

1.3kg/3lb ripe tomatoes, peeled, quartered and seeded

2 garlic cloves, finely chopped

salt and pepper

30ml/2 tbsp vegetable oil or butter

1 leek, chopped

1 carrot, chopped

1.2 litres/2 pints unsalted chicken stock

115g/4oz blue cheese, such as Oregon Blue, crumbled

45ml/3 tbsp whipping cream

several large fresh basil leaves, or 1–2 fresh parsley sprigs

175g/6oz bacon, cooked and crumbled

1 Preheat oven to 200°C/400°F/ Gas 6.

2 ▲ Spread the tomatoes in a baking dish. Sprinkle with the garlic and some salt and pepper. Place in the oven and bake for 35 minutes.

3 ▲ Heat the oil or butter in a large pan. Add the leek and carrot and season lightly with salt and pepper. Cook over a low heat, stirring often, until softened, about 10 minutes.

4 ▲ Stir in the stock and tomatoes. Bring to the boil, then lower the heat, cover and simmer for 20 minutes.

5 ▲ Add the blue cheese, cream and basil or parsley. Transfer to a food processor or blender and process until smooth (work in batches if necessary). Taste for seasoning.

6 If necessary, reheat the soup, but do not boil. Ladle into bowls and sprinkle with the crumbled bacon.

Macaroni and Blue Cheese

SERVES 6

450g/1lb macaroni

1.2 litres/2 pints milk

50g/2oz/¼ cup butter

90ml/6 tbsp plain (all-purpose) flour

1.5ml/¼ tsp salt

225g/8oz blue cheese, such as
Oregon Blue, crumbled

black pepper, for serving

1 Preheat the oven to 180°C/350°F/Gas 4.
Grease a 33 × 23cm/13 × 9in baking dish.

2 ▲ Bring a large pan of water to the
boil. Salt to taste and add the macaroni.
Cook until just tender (check the
packet instructions for cooking times).
Drain and rinse under cold water.
Place in a large bowl. Set aside.

3 In another pan, bring the milk to
the boil and set aside.

4 ▲ Melt the butter in a heavy pan
over a low heat. Whisk in the flour and
cook for 5 minutes, whisking constantly;
do not let the mixture become brown.

5 ▼ Remove from the heat and whisk
the hot milk into the butter and flour
mixture. When the mixture is smoothly
blended, return to a medium heat and
continue cooking, whisking constantly,
until the sauce is thick, about 5 minutes.
Add the salt.

6 Add the sauce to the macaroni.
Add three-quarters of the crumbled
blue cheese and stir well. Transfer the
macaroni mixture to the prepared
baking dish and spread in an even layer.

7 Sprinkle the remaining cheese
evenly over the surface. Bake until
bubbling hot, about 25 minutes.

8 If you like, lightly brown the top of
the macaroni cheese under a hot grill
(broiler) for 3–4 minutes. Serve hot,
sprinkled with black pepper.

Smoked Trout Pasta Salad

SERVES 6

15g/½oz/1 tbsp butter

115g/4oz/1 cup finely chopped
    fennel bulb

6 spring onions (scallions),
    2 finely chopped and 4 thinly sliced

salt and pepper

225g/8oz skinless smoked trout
    fillets, flaked

45ml/3 tbsp chopped fresh dill

120ml/4fl oz/½ cup mayonnaise

10ml/2 tsp fresh lemon juice

30ml/2 tbsp whipping cream

450g/1lb small pasta shapes,
    such as shells

fresh dill sprigs, to garnish (optional)

1 ▼ Melt the butter in a small non-stick frying pan. Add the fennel and finely chopped spring onions and season lightly with salt and pepper. Cook over a medium heat until just softened, 3–5 minutes. Transfer to a large bowl and leave to cool slightly.

2 ▲ Add the sliced spring onions, trout, dill, mayonnaise, lemon juice and cream. Mix gently until well blended.

3 ▲ Bring a large pan of water to the boil. Salt to taste and add the pasta. Cook until just tender (check the packet intructions for cooking times). Drain thoroughly and leave to cool.

4 ▲ Add the pasta to the vegetable and trout mixture and toss to coat evenly. Taste for seasoning. Serve the salad lightly chilled or at room temperature, garnished with dill, if you like.

Trout and Bacon Hash

SERVES 2

3–4 potatoes, cut into 1cm/½in cubes

salt and pepper

40g/1½oz/3 tbsp unsalted butter

½ onion, finely chopped

½ green (bell) pepper, seeded and
finely chopped

1 garlic clove, finely chopped

50g/2oz Canadian bacon or other
back bacon, chopped

200g/7oz skinless trout fillets, cut into
1cm/½in pieces

5ml/1 tsp dried oregano

15ml/1 tbsp chopped fresh parsley
(optional)

3 ▼ Add the remaining butter and
the potatoes to the frying pan. Cook
over a high heat, stirring occasionally,
until the potatoes are lightly browned,
about 5 minutes longer.

4 ▲ Add the trout, oregano and
parsley, if using. Season with salt and
pepper. Continue cooking, smashing
down with a wooden spoon, until the
trout is cooked through, 3–4 minutes
more. Serve at once.

1 ▲ Put the potatoes in a pan, add
cold water to cover, and bring to the
boil. Add 5ml/1 tsp salt and simmer
until just tender, 8–10 minutes. Drain
and set aside.

2 ▲ Melt 25g/1oz/2 tbsp of the butter
in a large non-stick frying pan. Add
the onion, pepper, garlic and bacon
and cook over a medium heat until the
onion is just softened, 5–8 minutes.

Seattle Fish Fritters

SERVES 4

½ fennel bulb, finely chopped

1 medium leek, finely chopped

1 green (bell) pepper, seeded and diced

2 garlic cloves

15g/½oz/1 tbsp butter

pinch of red pepper flakes

salt and pepper

175g/6oz skinless salmon fillet,
    cut into pieces

90g/3½oz skinless rockfish fillet or
    ling cod, cut into pieces

75g/3oz cooked peeled prawns (shrimp)

115g/4oz/1 cup plain (all-purpose) flour

6 eggs, beaten

350–475ml/12–16fl oz/1½–2 cups milk

15ml/1 tbsp chopped fresh basil

60–90ml/4–6 tbsp oil, for greasing

sour cream, for serving

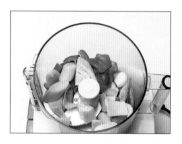

1 ▲ Combine the fennel, leek, pepper and garlic in a food processor and process until finely chopped.

~ VARIATION ~

For Seattle Salmon Fritters, increase the amount of salmon to 350g/12oz, and omit the rockfish or ling cod and prawns. Use dill in place of the basil. Serve with a tossed green salad, if you like.

2 ▲ Melt the butter in a frying pan until sizzling. Add the vegetable mixture and red pepper flakes. Season with salt and pepper. Cook over a low heat until softened, 8–10 minutes. Remove from the heat and set aside.

3 ▲ Place the salmon, rockfish or ling cod and prawns in the food processor. Process, using the pulse button and scraping the sides of the container several times, until the mixture is coarsely chopped. Scrape into a large bowl and set aside.

4 ▲ Sift the flour into another bowl and make a well in the centre.

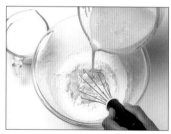

5 ▲ Gradually whisk in the eggs alternately with 350ml/12fl oz/1½ cups milk to make a smooth batter. Strain the batter to remove lumps, If necessary.

6 ▲ Stir the seafood, vegetables and basil into the batter. If it seems too thick, add a little more milk.

7 ▲ Lightly oil a griddle or non-stick frying pan and place over a medium heat. Ladle in the batter, adding around 75ml/2½fl oz/⅓ cup at a time. Cook the fritters until both sides are golden around the edges, 2–3 minutes per side. Work in batches, keeping the cooked fritters warm.

8 Serve hot, with sour cream.

Scalloped Oysters

90g/3½oz/7 tbsp butter
1 shallot, finely chopped
115g/4oz mushrooms, finely chopped
10ml/2 tsp plain (all-purpose) flour
dash of hot pepper sauce
salt and pepper
24 oysters, shucked and drained
75ml/2½fl oz/⅓ cup dry white wine
150ml/¼ pint/⅔ cup whipping cream
30ml/2 tbsp chopped fresh parsley
90ml/6 tbsp fresh breadcrumbs

1 Preheat the oven to 190°C/375°F/Gas 5. Grease a 15 × 20cm/6 × 8in baking dish.

2 Melt the butter in a large frying pan. Add the shallot and mushrooms and cook until softened, about 3 minutes.

3 ▼ Add the flour and hot pepper sauce. Season with salt and pepper. Cook, stirring constantly, for 1 minute.

4 ▲ Stir in the oysters and wine, scraping the bottom of the frying pan. Add the cream. Transfer the mixture to the prepared baking dish.

5 ▲ In a small bowl, combine the chopped parsley, fresh breadcrumbs and salt to taste. Stir to mix.

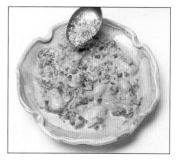

6 ▲ Sprinkle the crumbs evenly over the oyster mixture. Bake until the top is golden and the sauce bubbling, 15–20 minutes. Serve at once.

Penn Cove Steamed Mussels

SERVES 2

675g/1½lb mussels in shell

½ fennel bulb, finely chopped

1 shallot, finely chopped

45ml/3 tbsp dry white wine

45ml/3 tbsp whipping cream

30ml/2 tbsp chopped fresh parsley

black pepper

1 ▲ Scrub the mussels under cold running water. Remove any barnacles with a small knife, and remove the beards. Rinse once more.

2 ▲ Place the mussels in a large casserole with a lid. Sprinkle them with the fennel, shallot and wine. Cover the casserole and place over a medium-high heat. Steam until the mussels open, 3–5 minutes.

3 Lift out the mussels with a slotted spoon and remove the top shells. Discard any mussels that did not open. Arrange the mussels, on their bottom shells, in one layer in a shallow serving dish. Keep warm.

4 ▼ Place a double layer of dampened muslin (cheesecloth) in a strainer set over a bowl. Strain the mussel cooking liquid through the muslin. Return the strained liquid to a clean pan and bring to the boil.

5 ▲ Add the cream, stir well and boil for 3 minutes to reduce slightly. Stir in the parsley. Spoon the sauce over the mussels and sprinkle with freshly ground black pepper. Serve the mussels at once.

Stuffed Potato Skins

SERVES 6

3 baking potatoes, about 350g/12oz
  each, scrubbed and patted dry

15ml/1 tbsp vegetable oil

40g/1½oz/3 tbsp butter

1 onion, chopped

salt and pepper

1 green (bell) pepper, seeded and
  coarsely chopped

5ml/1 tsp paprika

115g/4oz/1 cup grated Monterey Jack or
  Cheddar cheese

1 Preheat oven to 230°C/450°F/Gas 8.

2 ▲ Brush the potatoes all over with
the oil. Prick them in several places
on all sides with a fork.

3 ▲ Place in a baking dish. Bake
until tender, about 1½ hours.

4 ▲ Meanwhile, heat the butter in a
large non-stick frying pan. Add the
onion and a little salt and cook over a
medium heat until softened, about
5 minutes. Add the pepper and
continue cooking until just tender but
still crunchy, 2–3 minutes more. Stir in
the paprika and set aside.

5 ▲ When the potatoes are done,
halve them lengthways. Scoop out the
flesh, keeping the pieces coarse. Keep
the potato skins warm.

6 Preheat the grill (broiler).

~ VARIATION ~

For Bacon-stuffed Potato Skins, add
130g/4½oz/¾ cup chopped cooked
bacon to the cooked potato flesh
and vegetables. Stuff as above.

7 ▲ Add the potato flesh to the
frying pan and cook over a high heat,
stirring, until the potato is lightly
browned. Season with pepper.

8 ▲ Divide the vegetable mixture
between the potato skins.

9 ▲ Sprinkle the cheese on top.
Grill until the cheese just melts,
3–5 minutes. Serve at once.

Pasta with Scallops

SERVES 4

450g/1lb pasta, such as fettucine
    or linguine

30ml/2 tbsp olive oil

2 garlic cloves, finely chopped

450g/1lb scallops,
    sliced in half horizontally

salt and pepper

FOR THE SAUCE

30ml/2 tbsp olive oil

½ onion, finely chopped

1 garlic clove, finely chopped

2.5ml/½ tsp salt

2 × 400g/14oz cans peeled tomatoes
    in juice

30ml/2 tbsp chopped fresh basil

1 For the sauce, heat the oil in a non-stick frying pan. Add the onion, garlic and a little salt, and cook over a medium heat until just softened, about 5 minutes, stirring occasionally.

2 ▲ Add the tomatoes, with their juice, and crush with the tines of a fork. Bring to the boil, then reduce the heat and simmer gently for 15 minutes. Remove from the heat and set aside.

3 ▲ Bring a large pan of salted water to the boil. Add the pasta and cook until just tender to the bite (check the packet instructions for cooking times).

4 ▲ Meanwhile, combine the oil and garlic in another non-stick frying pan and cook until just sizzling, about 30 seconds. Add the scallops and 2.5ml/½ tsp salt and cook over a high heat, tossing, until the scallops are cooked through, about 3 minutes.

5 ▲ Add the scallops to the tomato sauce. Season with salt and pepper, stir and keep warm.

6 Drain the pasta, rinse under hot water and drain again. Place in a large warmed serving bowl. Add the scallop sauce and the basil and toss thoroughly. Serve at once.

Clam and Sausage Chilli

SERVES 4

185g/6½oz/1 cup dried black kidney beans, soaked overnight and drained

1 bay leaf

2.5ml/½ tsp sea salt

225g/½lb lean pork sausage meat (bulk sausage)

15ml/1 tbsp vegetable oil

1 onion, finely chopped

1 garlic clove, finely chopped

5ml/1 tsp fennel seeds

5ml/1 tsp dried oregano

1.5ml/¼ tsp red pepper flakes, or to taste

10–15ml/2–3 tsp chilli powder, or to taste

5ml/1 tsp ground cumin

2 × 400g/14oz cans canned chopped tomatoes in juice

120ml/4fl oz/½ cup dry white wine

2 × 275g/10oz cans clams, drained and liquid reserved

salt and pepper

1 Put the beans in a large pan. Add fresh cold water to cover and the bay leaf. Bring to the boil, then cover and simmer for 30 minutes. Add the salt and continue simmering until tender, about 30 minutes more. Drain the beans and discard the bay leaf.

2 ▲ Put the sausage meat in a large flameproof casserole. Cook over a medium heat until just beginning to brown, 2–3 minutes. Stir frequently to break up the lumps. Add the oil, onion and garlic.

3 Continue cooking until the vegetables are softened, about 5 minutes more, stirring occasionally.

4 ▼ Stir in the herbs and spices, tomatoes, wine and 150ml/¼ pint/⅔ cup of the reserved clam juice. Bring to the boil, then lower the heat and cook, stirring occasionally, for 15 minutes.

5 ▲ Add the black beans and clams and stir to combine. Taste and adjust the seasoning if necessary. Continue cooking until the clams are just heated through. Serve at once.

Pan-fried Trout with Horseradish Sauce

<u>SERVES 4</u>

4 whole rainbow trout, about 175g/6oz each, cleaned

salt and pepper

25g/1oz/¼ cup plain (all-purpose) flour

25g/1oz/2 tbsp butter

15ml/1 tbsp vegetable oil

<u>FOR THE SAUCE</u>

120ml/4fl oz/½ cup mayonnaise

120ml/4fl oz/½ cup sour cream

3.5ml/¾ tsp grated horseradish

1.5ml/¼ tsp paprika

30ml/2 tbsp tomato or lemon juice

15ml/1 tbsp chopped fresh herbs, such as chives, parsley or basil

1 ▼ For the sauce, combine the mayonnaise, sour cream, horseradish, paprika, tomato or lemon juice and herbs. Season with salt and pepper and mix well. Set the sauce aside.

2 ▲ Rinse the trout and pat dry. Season the cavities in the fish generously with salt and pepper.

3 ▲ Combine the flour, 2.5ml/½ tsp salt and a little pepper in a shallow dish. Coat the trout on both sides with the seasoned flour, shaking off any excess.

4 ▲ Heat the butter and oil in a large non-stick frying pan over a medium-high heat. When sizzling, add the trout and cook until opaque throughout, 4–5 minutes on each side. Serve at once, with the sauce.

Salmon with Sizzling Herbs

SERVES 4

4 salmon steaks, 175–200g/6–7oz each

salt and pepper

75ml/2½fl oz/⅓ cup olive oil

25g/1 oz/½ cup chopped fresh
  coriander (cilantro)

45ml/3 tbsp finely chopped fresh root ginger

40g/1½oz/½ cup chopped spring
  onions (scallions)

50ml/2fl oz/¼ cup soy sauce, plus extra
  for serving

1 Bring some water to the boil in the
bottom of a steamer.

2 ▲ Season the fish steaks on both
sides with salt and pepper.

3 ▲ Place the fish steaks in the top
part of the steamer. Cover the pan
and steam until the fish is opaque
throughout, 7–8 minutes.

4 ▼ Meanwhile, heat the oil in a
small heavy pan until very hot. (To
test the temperature, drop in a piece of
chopped spring onion; if it sizzles, the
oil is hot enough.)

5 Place the steamed salmon steaks on
warmed plates.

6 ▲ Divide the chopped coriander
among the salmon steaks, heaping it
on top of the fish. Sprinkle with the
ginger and then the spring onions.
Drizzle 15ml/1 tbsp of the soy sauce
over each salmon steak.

7 Spoon the hot oil over each salmon
steak and serve at once, with additional
soy sauce.

Pork Chops with Cider and Apples

SERVES 4

450g/1lb tart cooking apples (3–4), peeled, quartered and cored

4 pork chops, about 2.5cm/1in thick

5ml/1 tsp dried thyme

1.5ml/¼ tsp ground allspice

salt and pepper

15g/½oz/1 tbsp butter

15ml/1 tbsp vegetable oil

1 bay leaf

120ml/4fl oz/½ cup apple cider

30ml/2 tbsp whipping cream

potato pancakes, for serving

1 Preheat the oven to 190°C/375°F/ Gas 5. Grease a casserole large enough to hold the pork chops in one layer.

2 ▲ Spread the apples in an even layer in the prepared dish. Set aside.

3 Sprinkle the pork chops on both sides with the thyme, ground allspice and a little salt and pepper.

4 Heat the butter and oil in a frying pan. When hot, add the pork chops and cook over a medium-high heat until browned, 2–3 minutes. Turn and cook the other side, 2–3 minutes more. Remove from the heat.

5 ▲ Arrange the pork chops on top of the apples. Add the bay leaf and pour over the cider. Cover and bake for 15 minutes.

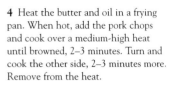

6 ▲ Turn the chops over. Continue baking until they are cooked through, about 15 minutes more.

7 Transfer the pork chops to warmed plates. Remove the apple quarters with a slotted spoon and divide them equally among the plates.

8 Stir the cream into the sauce and heat just until warmed through. Taste for seasoning. Spoon the sauce over the pork chops and serve at once, with potato pancakes.

Pork Braised in Beer

SERVES 6

1.8–2.25kg/4–5lb pork loin, boned, trimmed of excess fat and tied into a neat shape

salt and pepper

15ml/1 tbsp butter

15ml/1 tbsp vegetable oil

3 large onions, halved and thinly sliced

1 garlic clove, finely chopped

750ml/1¼ pints/3 cups beer

1 bay leaf

15ml/1 tbsp plain (all-purpose) flour blended with 30ml/2 tbsp water

3 ▲ Stir in the beer, scraping to remove any bits on the bottom of the pan. Add the bay leaf.

4 Return the pork to the casserole. Cover and cook over a low heat for about 2 hours, turning the pork halfway through the cooking time.

5 ▼ Remove the pork. Cut it into serving slices and arrange on a serving dish. Cover and keep warm.

6 Discard the bay leaf. Add the flour to the cooking juices and cook over a high heat, stirring constantly, until thickened. Taste for seasoning. Pour the sauce over the pork slices and serve at once.

1 ▲ Season the pork loin on all sides with salt and pepper. Heat the butter and oil in a flameproof casserole just large enough to hold the pork loin. When hot, add the meat and brown on all sides, 5–7 minutes, turning it to colour evenly. Remove from the casserole and set aside.

2 ▲ Drain the excess fat from the pan, leaving about 15ml/1 tbsp. Add the onions and garlic and cook just until softened, about 5 minutes.

Chicken and Mushroom Pie

SERVES 6

15g/½ oz dried porcini mushrooms

50g/2oz/¼ cup butter

30ml/2 tbsp plain (all-purpose) flour

250ml/8fl oz/1 cup chicken stock, warmed

50ml/2fl oz/¼ cup whipping cream or milk

salt and pepper

1 onion, coarsely chopped

2 carrots, sliced

2 celery sticks, coarsely chopped

50g/2oz mushrooms, quartered

450g/1lb cooked chicken meat, cubed

50g/2oz/½ cup shelled fresh or frozen peas

beaten egg, for glazing

FOR THE PASTRY

225g/8oz/2 cups plain (all-purpose) flour

1.5ml/¼ tsp salt

75g/3oz/6 tbsp cold butter, diced

25g/1oz/2 tbsp lard or white cooking
fat, diced

45–60ml/3–4 tbsp iced water

1 ▲ For the pastry, sift the flour and salt into a bowl. With a pastry blender, cut in the butter and lard or white cooking fat until the mixture resembles breadcrumbs, or rub in with your fingertips. Sprinkle with 45ml/3 tbsp of the iced water and mix until the pastry holds together. If it is too crumbly, add a little more water, 5ml/1 tsp at a time. Gather the pastry into a ball and flatten into a disk. Wrap in clear film (plastic wrap) and chill for at least 30 minutes.

2 Place the porcini mushrooms in a small bowl. Add hot water to cover and soak until soft, about 30 minutes. Lift out of the water with a slotted spoon to leave any grit behind and drain. Discard the soaking water.

3 Preheat oven to 190°C/375°F/Gas 5.

4 ▲ Melt half the butter in a heavy pan. Whisk in the flour and cook until bubbling, whisking constantly. Add the warm chicken stock and cook over a medium heat, whisking, until the mixture boils. Cook for 2–3 minutes more. Whisk in the whipping cream or milk. Season with salt and pepper. Set aside.

5 ▲ Heat the remaining butter in a large non-stick frying pan until foamy. Add the onion and carrots and cook until softened, about 5 minutes. Add the celery and fresh mushrooms and cook for 5 minutes more. Stir in the chicken, peas and drained porcini mushrooms.

6 Add the chicken mixture to the cream sauce and stir to mix. Taste for seasoning. Transfer to a 2.5 litre/4 pint/10 cup rectangular baking dish.

7 ▲ Roll out the pastry to about 3mm/⅛in thick. Cut out a rectangle about 2.5cm/1in larger all around than the dish. Lay the rectangle of pastry over the filling. Make a decorative edge, crimping the pastry by pushing the index finger of one hand between the thumb and index finger of the other.

8 Cut several vents in the pastry to allow steam to escape. Brush with the egg glaze.

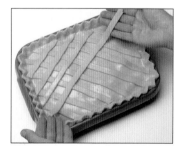

9 ▲ Press together the dough trimmings, then roll out again. Cut into strips and lay them over the top crust. Glaze again. If desired, roll small balls of dough and set them in the "windows" in the lattice.

10 Bake until the pastry is browned, about 30 minutes. Serve the pie hot from the dish.

Oregon Blue Cheese Burgers

SERVES 4

900g/2lb lean beef mince

1 garlic clove, finely chopped

30ml/2 tbsp chopped fresh parsley

30ml/2 tbsp chopped fresh chives

2.5ml/½ tsp salt

pepper

225g/8oz Oregon Blue cheese, crumbled

4 hamburger buns, split and toasted

TO SERVE

tomato slices and lettuce

mustard or ketchup

1 ▼ In a bowl, combine the beef, garlic, parsley, chives, salt and a little pepper. Mix lightly together, then form into four thick burgers.

2 ▲ Make a slit in the side of each burger, poking well into the beef to form a pocket. Fill each pocket with 50g/2oz of the blue cheese.

3 ▲ Close the holes to seal the blue cheese inside the burgers.

4 Heat a ridged frying pan or preheat the grill (broiler).

5 Cook the burgers for 4–5 minutes on each side for medium-rare, about 6–7 minutes for well done.

6 ▲ Place the burgers in the split hamburger buns. Serve at once, with sliced tomatoes and lettuce leaves, and mustard or ketchup if you like.

Steak with Mushrooms and Leeks in Red Wine

SERVES 4

6–8 leeks (about 500g/1¼lb), white and light green parts only

50ml/2fl oz/¼ cup olive oil

675g/1½lb mushrooms, quartered

475ml/16fl oz/2 cups dry red wine, such as a pinot noir or merlot

salt and pepper

4 × 225g/8oz boneless sirloin steaks, about 2cm/¾in thick

15ml/1 tbsp chopped fresh parsley

4 Remove the lid, raise the heat and cook until the wine has reduced slightly, about 5 minutes. Set aside.

5 ▼ Brush the steaks with the remaining 15ml/1 tbsp oil and sprinkle generously on both sides with salt and pepper.

6 Heat a ridged frying pan or preheat the grill (broiler). When hot, add the steaks and cook for 3–4 minutes on each side for medium-rare.

7 Meanwhile, stir the parsley into the leek mixture and reheat.

8 Place the steaks on four warmed plates. Heap the leek mixture on top and serve.

> **~ VARIATION ~**
>
> If available, use fresh wild mushrooms for extra flavour.

1 ▲ Trim the leeks and cut into 2.5cm/1in slices on the diagonal.

2 ▲ Heat 45ml/3 tbsp of the oil in a large frying pan. When hot, add the leeks and mushrooms and cook over a medium heat, stirring often, until lightly browned.

3 Stir in the wine, scraping the bottom of the pan. Season with salt and pepper. Bring to the boil and boil for 1 minute. Reduce the heat to low, then cover and cook for 5 minutes.

Idaho Beef Stew

SERVES 6

50ml/2fl oz/¼ cup vegetable oil

2 onions, chopped

4 large carrots, thickly sliced

1.3kg/3lb chuck steak, cubed

salt and pepper

45ml/3 tbsp plain (all-purpose) flour

750ml/1¼ pints/3 cups unsalted beef stock

250ml/8fl oz/1 cup strong black coffee

10ml/2 tsp dried oregano

1 bay leaf

115g/4oz/1 cup shelled fresh or frozen peas

mashed potatoes, for serving

1 ▼ Heat 30ml/2 tbsp of the oil in a large flameproof casserole. Add the onions and carrots and cook over a medium heat until lightly browned, about 8 minutes. Remove them with a slotted spoon, transfer to a plate or dish and reserve.

2 ▲ Add another 15ml/1 tbsp of the oil to the casserole and then add the beef cubes. Raise the heat to medium-high and cook until browned all over. (Work in batches if necessary.) Season with salt and pepper.

3 ▲ Return the vegetables to the casserole. Add the flour and the remaining 15ml/1 tbsp of oil. Cook, stirring constantly, for 1 minute. Add the stock, coffee, oregano and bay leaf. Bring to the boil and cook, stirring often, until thickened. Reduce the heat to low, then cover the casserole and simmer gently until the beef is tender, about 45 minutes.

4 ▲ Add the peas and simmer for 5–10 minutes more. Discard the bay leaf and taste for seasoning. Serve hot, with mashed potatoes.

Pot-Roasted Veal Chops with Carrots

SERVES 4

15ml/1 tbsp vegetable oil

15g/½oz/1 tbsp butter

4 veal chops, about 2cm/¾in thick

salt and pepper

1 onion, halved and thinly sliced

120ml/4fl oz/½ cup dry white wine

675g/1½lb carrots, cut into 1cm/½in slices

1 bay leaf

120ml/4fl oz/½ cup whipping cream

1 Preheat the oven to 180°C/350°F/ Gas 4.

2 ▲ Heat the oil and butter in a flameproof casserole large enough to hold the veal chops in one layer. Add the chops and cook over a medium heat until well browned on both sides, 6–8 minutes. Transfer to a plate, season with salt and pepper and set aside.

3 ▲ Add the onion to the pan and cook until it is just softened, about 5 minutes. Stir in the wine.

4 ▼ Return the veal chops to the pan. Add the carrots. Season with salt and pepper and add the bay leaf.

5 Cover the casserole and transfer it to the oven. Cook until the chops are tender, about 30 minutes.

6 Remove the chops and carrots to warm plates and keep warm. Discard the bay leaf. Stir the cream into the cooking liquid and bring to the boil. Simmer until the sauce is slightly thickened, 2–3 minutes.

7 Taste the sauce and adjust the seasoning if necessary, then spoon it over the chops. Serve at once.

Cauliflower au Gratin

SERVES 4

1.2kg/2½lb cauliflower florets
  (about 1 large head)

40g/1½oz/3 tbsp butter

45ml/3 tbsp plain (all-purpose) flour

475ml/16fl oz/2 cups milk

50g/2oz/½ cup grated mature (sharp)
  Cheddar cheese

salt and pepper

3 bay leaves

1 ▲ Preheat the oven to 180°C/350°F/
Gas 4. Grease a 30cm/12in baking dish.

2 Bring a large pan of salted water
to the boil. Add the cauliflower and
cook until just tender but still firm,
7–8 minutes. Drain well.

3 ▲ Melt the butter in a heavy pan.
Whisk in the flour until thoroughly
blended and cook until bubbling.
Gradually add the milk. Bring to the
boil and continue cooking, stirring
constantly, until thick.

4 ▲ Remove from the heat and stir
in the grated cheese. Season the sauce
with salt and pepper.

5 ▲ Place the bay leaves on the
bottom of the prepared dish. Arrange
the cauliflower florets on top in an
even layer. Pour the cheese sauce
evenly over the cauliflower.

6 Bake until browned, 20–25 minutes.
Serve at once.

Wild Rice Pilaff

SERVES 6

200g/7oz/1 cup wild rice

salt and pepper

40g/1½oz/3 tbsp butter

½ onion, finely chopped

200g/7oz/1 cup long grain rice

475ml/16fl oz/2 cups chicken stock

65g/2½oz/⅔ cup flaked (sliced) almonds

90g/3½oz/⅔ cup sultanas (golden raisins)

30ml/2 tbsp chopped fresh parsley

3 Stir in the stock and bring to the boil. Cover and simmer gently until the rice is tender and the liquid has been absorbed, 30–40 minutes.

4 ▼ Melt the remaining butter in a small frying pan. Add the almonds and cook, stirring, until they are just golden, 2–3 minutes. Set aside.

5 ▲ In a large bowl, combine the wild rice, long grain rice, sultanas, almonds and parsley. Stir to mix. Taste and adjust the seasoning, if necessary. Transfer to a warmed serving dish and serve at once.

1 ▲ Bring a large pan of water to the boil. Add the wild rice and 15ml/1 tsp salt. Cover and simmer gently until the rice is tender, 45–60 minutes. When done, drain well.

2 ▲ Meanwhile, melt 15g/½oz/1 tbsp of the butter in another pan. Add the onion and cook over a medium heat until it is just softened, about 5 minutes. Stir in the long grain rice and cook for 1 minute more.

Blue Cheese and Chive Pennies

MAKES 48

225g/8oz blue cheese, such as
  Oregon Blue, crumbled

115g/4oz/½ cup unsalted butter,
  at room temperature

1 egg plus 1 egg yolk

45ml/3 tbsp chopped fresh chives

black pepper

225g/8oz/2 cups plain (all-purpose)
  flour, sifted

1 ▼ The day before serving, beat the
cheese and butter together until well
blended. Add the egg, egg yolk, chives
and a little pepper and beat just until
the ingredients are blended.

2 ▲ Add the flour in three batches,
folding in well between each addition.

3 ▲ Divide the mixture in half
and shape each half into a log about
5cm/2in in diameter. Wrap in baking
parchment and chill overnight.

4 Preheat the oven to 190°C/375°F/
Gas 5. Lightly grease two baking sheets.

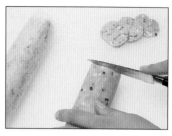

5 ▲ Cut the logs across into slices
about 3mm/⅛in thick. Place on the
prepared sheets.

6 Bake until just golden around the
edges, about 10 minutes. Transfer to a
wire rack to cool.

~ COOK'S TIP ~

The cheese pennies will keep for up
to 10 days in an airtight container.

Smoked Salmon and Dill Spread

MAKES 750ML/1¼ PINTS/3 CUPS

225g/8oz/1 cup ricotta cheese

225g/8oz/1 cup cream cheese,
  at room temperature

175g/6oz smoked salmon,
  finely chopped

115g/4oz cooked salmon, flaked

15g/½oz/¼ cup chopped fresh dill

45–60ml/3–4 tbsp fresh lemon juice

salt and pepper

vegetables, such as cucumber slices,
  Belgian endive leaves, (bell) pepper
  strips, or small toasts, for serving

1 ▲ Place the ricotta cheese, cream
cheese and smoked salmon in a food
processor or blender and process until
light and fluffy. Scrape the mixture
into a bowl.

2 ▼ Stir in the cooked salmon, dill
and 45ml/3 tbsp of the lemon juice.
Season with salt and pepper. Taste
and add the remaining lemon juice, if
you like. Serve the spread cold.

Blue Cheese and Chive Pennies (top), Smoked Salmon and Dill Spread

Winter Warmer (Hot White Chocolate)

SERVES 4

175g/6oz white chocolate

1.75 litres/3 pints/½ quarts milk

5ml/1 tsp coffee extract, or 10ml/2 tsp instant coffee powder

10ml/2 tsp orange-flavoured liqueur (optional)

TO SERVE

whipped cream

ground cinnamon

~ COOK'S TIP ~

If you prefer, use milk chocolate or plain (semisweet) chocolate instead of white chocolate, but taste before serving in case a little sugar is needed.

1 ▼ With a sharp knife, finely chop the white chocolate. (Try not to handle it too much or it will soften and stick together.)

2 Pour the milk into a medium heavy pan and bring just to the boil (bubbles will form around the edge of the pan).

3 ▲ Add the chopped white chocolate, coffee extract or powder and orange-flavoured liqueur, if using. Stir until the chocolate has melted.

4 Divide the hot chocolate between four coffee mugs. Top each with a rosette or spoonful of whipped cream and a sprinkling of ground cinnamon. Serve at once.

Easy Hazelnut Fudge

MAKES 16 SQUARES

150ml/¼ pint/⅔ cup evaporated milk

375g/13oz/1¾ cups granulated sugar

pinch of salt

50g/2oz/½ cup halved hazelnuts

350g/12oz/2 cups plain (semisweet) chocolate chips

5ml/1 tsp hazelnut liqueur (optional)

1 Generously grease a 20cm/8in square cake tin (pan).

~ VARIATION ~

For Easy Peanut Butter Fudge, substitute peanut butter chips for the chocolate chips and replace the hazelnuts with peanuts.

2 Combine the evaporated milk, sugar and salt in a heavy pan. Bring to the boil over a medium heat, stirring constantly. Simmer gently, stirring, for about 5 minutes.

3 ▼ Remove from the heat and add the hazelnuts, chocolate chips and liqueur, if using. Stir until the chocolate has completely melted.

4 ▲ Quickly pour the fudge mixture into the prepared pan and spread it out evenly. leave to cool.

5 When the fudge is set, cut it into 2.5cm/1in squares. Store in an airtight container, separating the layers with baking parchment.

Winter Warmer (top), Easy Hazelnut Fudge

Northwestern Brown Betty

SERVES 6

1kg/2¼lb pears (about 8)

50ml/2fl oz/¼ cup lemon juice

175g/6oz/3 cups fresh breadcrumbs

75g/3oz/6 tbsp butter, melted

90g/3½oz/⅔ cup dried cherries

65g/2½oz/⅔ cup coarsely
   chopped hazelnuts

90g/3½oz/½ cup soft light brown sugar

15–25g/½–1oz/1–2 tbsp butter,
   finely diced

whipped cream, for serving

1 Preheat the oven to 190°C/375°F/Gas 5. Grease a 20cm/8in square cake tin (pan).

2 ▼ Peel, core and dice the pears. Sprinkle them with the lemon juice to prevent discolouration.

3 ▲ Combine the breadcrumbs and melted butter in a bowl. Spread a scant one-third of the crumb mixture over the bottom of the prepared dish.

4 ▲ Top with half the pears. Sprinkle over half the dried cherries, half the hazelnuts and half the sugar. Repeat the layers, then finish with a layer of buttered breadcrumbs.

5 ▲ Dot with the pieces of butter. Bake until golden, 30–35 minutes. Serve hot, with whipped cream.

Rhubarb and Strawberry Crisp

SERVES 4

225g/8oz strawberries, hulled

450g/1lb rhubarb, diced

90g/3½oz/½ cup granulated sugar

15ml/1 tbsp cornflour (cornstarch)

75ml/2½fl oz/⅓ cup fresh orange juice

115g/4oz/1 cup plain (all-purpose) flour

90g/3½oz/1 cup rolled oats

90g/3½oz/½ cup soft light brown sugar

2.5ml/½ tsp ground cinnamon

50g/2oz/½ cup ground almonds

150g/5oz/10 tbsp cold butter, diced

1 egg, lightly beaten

1 Preheat oven to 180°C/350°F/Gas 4.

2 ▲ If the strawberries are large, cut them in half. Combine the strawberries, rhubarb and granulated sugar in a 2.5 litre/4 pint baking dish.

3 ▲ In a small bowl, blend the cornflour with the orange juice. Pour this mixture over the fruit and stir gently to coat. Set the baking dish aside while making the topping.

4 ▼ In a bowl, toss together the flour, oats, brown sugar, cinnamon and almonds. With a pastry blender, cut in the butter until the mixture resembles breadcrumbs, or rub in with your fingertips. Stir in the beaten egg.

5 ▲ Spoon the oat mixture evenly over the fruit and press down gently. Bake until browned, 50–60 minutes. Serve the crisp warm.

Blackberry Cobbler

SERVES 8

800g/1¾lb/6 cups blackberries

200g/7oz/1 cup granulated sugar

45ml/3 tbsp plain (all-purpose) flour

grated rind of 1 lemon

30ml/2 tbsp granulated sugar mixed with
   1.5ml/¼ tsp grated nutmeg

FOR THE TOPPING

225g/8oz/2 cups plain (all-purpose) flour

200g/7oz/1 cup granulated sugar

15ml/1 tbsp baking powder

pinch of salt

250ml/8fl oz/1 cup milk

115g/4oz/½ cup butter, melted

1 Preheat oven to 180°C/350°F/Gas 4.

2 ▼ In a bowl, combine the blackberries, sugar, flour and lemon rind. Stir gently to blend. Transfer to a 2.5 litre/4 pint baking dish.

3 ▲ For the topping, sift the flour, sugar, baking powder and salt into a large bowl. Set aside. In a measuring jug (cup), combine the milk and butter.

4 ▲ Gradually stir the milk mixture into the dry ingredients and stir until the mixture is just smooth.

5 ▲ Spoon the mixture over the berries, spreading to the edges.

6 Sprinkle the surface with the sugar and nutmeg mixture. Bake until the topping is set and lightly browned, about 50 minutes. Serve hot.

Baked Apples

SERVES 6

115g/4oz/½ cup chopped dried apricots

25g/1oz/½ cup chopped walnuts

5ml/1 tsp grated lemon rind

1.5ml/¼ tsp ground cinnamon

90g/3½oz/½ cup soft light brown sugar

25g/1oz/2 tbsp butter,
    at room temperature

6 baking apples

15ml/1 tbsp melted butter

1 Preheat oven to 190°C/375°F/Gas 5.

2 ▲ In a bowl, combine the apricots, walnuts, lemon rind and cinnamon. Add the sugar and butter and stir until thoroughly combined.

3 ▲ Core the apples, without cutting all the way through to the base. With a small knife, slightly widen the top of each opening by about 4cm/1½in to make room for the filling.

4 Spoon the apricot and walnut filling into the opening in the apples, packing it down lightly.

5 ▼ Place the apples in a baking dish just large enough to hold them comfortably side by side.

6 ▲ Brush the apples with the melted butter. Bake until they are tender, 40–45 minutes. Serve hot.

Blueberry and Hazelnut Cheesecake

SERVES 6–8

350g/12oz blueberries

15ml/1 tbsp honey

75g/3oz/6 tbsp granulated sugar

5ml/1 tsp plus 15ml/1 tbsp fresh
lemon juice

175g/6oz cream cheese,
at room temperature

1 egg

5ml/1 tsp hazelnut liqueur (optional)

120ml/4fl oz/½ cup whipping cream

FOR THE BISCUIT CASE

185g/6½oz/1⅔ cups ground hazelnuts

75g/3oz/⅔ cup plain (all-purpose) flour

pinch of salt

50g/2oz/¼ cup butter,
at room temperature

65g/2½oz/⅓ cup soft light brown sugar

1 egg yolk

1 ▲ For the crust, put the hazelnuts
in a large bowl. Sift in the flour and
salt, and stir to mix. Set aside.

~ COOK'S TIP ~

The cheesecake can be prepared
1 day in advance, but add the fruit
shortly before serving. Instead of
covering the top completely, leave
spaces to make a design, if you wish.

2 Beat the butter with the brown
sugar until light and fluffy. Beat in the
egg yolk. Gradually fold in the nut
mixture, in three batches.

3 ▲ Press the biscuit mixture into a
greased 23cm/9in pie dish, spreading it
evenly against the sides. Form a rim
around the top edge that is slightly
thicker than the sides. Cover and chill
for at least 30 minutes.

4 Preheat oven to 180°C/350°F/Gas 4.

5 ▲ Meanwhile, for the topping,
combine the blueberries, honey,
15ml/1 tbsp of the granulated sugar
and 5ml/1 tsp lemon juice in a heavy
pan. Cook the mixture over a low
heat, stirring occasionally, until the
berries have given off some liquid but
still retain their shape, 5–7 minutes.
Remove from the heat and set aside.

6 Place the base in the oven and
bake for 15 minutes. Remove and leave
to cool while making the filling.

7 ▲ Beat together the cream cheese
and remaining granulated sugar until
light and fluffy. Add the egg,
remaining lemon juice, the liqueur,
if using, and the cream and beat until
thoroughly incorporated.

8 ▲ Pour the cheese mixture into
the crust and spread evenly. Bake
until just set, 20–25 minutes.

9 Let the cheesecake cool completely
on a wire rack, then cover and chill for
at least 1 hour.

10 Spread the blueberry mixture
evenly over the top of the cheesecake.
Serve at cool room temperature.

Mocha Vanilla Deserts

SERVES 6

285g/10½oz/1½ cups granulated sugar

90ml/6 tbsp cornflour (cornstarch)

1 litre/1¾ pints/4 cups milk

3 egg yolks

75g/3oz/6 tbsp unsalted butter,
  at room temperature

20ml/4 tsp instant coffee powder

10ml/2 tsp vanilla extract

30ml/2 tbsp unsweetened cocoa powder

whipped cream, for serving

1 ▲ For the coffee layer, combine 90g/
3½oz/½ cup of the sugar and 30ml/2 tbsp
of the cornflour in a heavy pan. Gradually
add 325ml/11fl oz/1⅓ cups of the milk,
whisking until well blended. Over a
medium heat, whisk in one egg yolk
and bring to the boil, whisking constantly.
Boil for 1 minute, still whisking.

2 ▲ Remove from the heat. Stir in
30ml/2 tbsp of the butter and the
coffee powder. Leave to cool slightly.

3 ▲ Divide the coffee mixture
among six wine glasses. Smooth the
tops before the mixture sets.

4 ▲ Wipe any dribbles on the insides
and outsides of the glasses with damp
kitchen paper.

5 ▲ For the vanilla layer, combine 90g/
3½oz/½ cup of the sugar and 30ml/2 tbsp
of the cornflour in a heavy pan. Gradually
whisk in 325ml/11fl oz/1⅓ cups of the milk
until well blended. Over a medium heat,
whisk in one egg yolk and bring to the
boil, whisking. Boil for 1 minute.

6 Remove from the heat and stir in
25g/1oz/2 tbsp of the butter and the
vanilla. Leave to cool slightly, then
spoon into the glasses on top of the
coffee layer. Smooth the tops and wipe
the glasses with kitchen paper.

7 ▲ For the chocolate layer, combine
the remaining sugar and cornflour in a
heavy pan. Gradually whisk in the
remaining milk until well blended.
Over a moderate heat, whisk in the
last egg yolk and bring to the boil,
whisking constantly. Boil for 1 minute.
Off the heat, stir in the remaining
butter and the cocoa powder. Leave to
cool slightly, then spoon into the
glasses on top of the vanilla layer.
Chill until set.

8 ▲ Pipe or spoon whipped cream on
top of each pudding before serving.

~ COOK'S TIP ~

For a special occasion, prepare the
vanilla layer using a fresh vanilla
pod (bean). Choose a plump, supple
pod and split it down the centre
with a sharp knife. Add to the
mixture with the milk and discard
the pod before spooning into the
glasses. The flavour will be more
pronounced and the pudding will
have pretty brown speckles from
the vanilla seeds.

Index

~

A

acorn squash: baked acorn
squash with herbs, 110
caramel-baked acorn
squash, 110
apples: apple brown Betty, 41
apple fritters, 122
apple maple dumplings, 121
applesauce cookies, 126
baked apples, 247
baked pork loin with red
cabbage and apples, 106
pork chops with cider and
apples, 230
Arizona jalapeño-onion
quiche, 134
artichoke pasta salad, 180
asparagus: asparagus with
creamy raspberry
vinaigrette, 181
chilled asparagus soup, 11
avocado: avocado dressing,
204
guacamole, 156
lemon chicken with
guacamole sauce, 190
Miami chilled avocado
soup, 50
Palm Beach papaya and
avocado salad, 52
Sante Fe shrimp salad, 136
turkey and avocado pita
pizzas, 175

B

bacon: bacon-stuffed potato
skins, 224
cheddar and bacon biscuits,
112
dandelion salad with hot
bacon dressing, 94
tomato-blue cheese soup
with bacon, 216
trout and bacon hash, 219
warm salad of black-eyed
peas, 53
baked acorn squash with
herbs, 110
baked apples, 247
baked beans, Boston, 32
baked peaches with raspberry
sauce, 207
baked pork loin with red
cabbage and apples, 106

baked scrod, 20
bananas: banana lemon layer
cake, 83
chocolate cinnamon cake
with banana sauce, 162
Mexican hot fudge
sundaes, 164
basil: Cajun "popcorn" with
basil mayonnaise, 57
roast leg of lamb with
pesto, 197
beans: bean dip, 161
black bean burritos, 140
black bean chili, 141
Boston baked beans, 32
huevos rancheros, 132
pinto bean salad, 137
spicy bean soup, 131
three-bean and lentil salad,
179
beef: beef and eggplant stir-
fry with ginger, 198
beef enchiladas, 152
California taco salad with
beef, 182
country meat loaf, 104
Idaho beef stew, 236
Indian beef and berry soup,
92
lone star steak and potato
dinner, 154
Oregon blue cheese
burgers, 234
red flannel hash with
corned beef, 30
spicy sauerbraten with
gingersnap gravy, 108
steak with mushrooms and
leeks in red wine, 235
tamale pie, 151
twin cities meatballs, 103
Yankee pot roast, 28
beer: pork braised in beer,
231
beets: Harvard beets, 32
pickled eggs and beets, 116
red flannel hash with
corned beef, 31
beignets: French Quarter
beignets, 79
bell peppers: chiles rellenos,
138
swordfish with bell pepper-
orange relish, 186
warm salad of black-eyed
peas, 53

berries: berry salsa, 200
Indian beef and berry soup,
92
Shaker summer pudding, 40
see also blackberries;
blueberries, etc.
biscuits: cheddar and bacon
biscuits, 112
cornmeal biscuits, 78
sausage gravy on biscuits,
102
sweet potato biscuits, 37
Wisconsin cheddar and
chive biscuits, 112
black beans: black bean
burritos, 140
black bean chili, 141
spicy bean soup, 131
black-eyed peas: warm salad
of black-eyed peas, 53
black walnut layer cake, 124
blackberries: blackberry
cobbler, 246
Indian beef and berry soup,
92
Shaker summer pudding, 40
blackened catfish fillets, 71
blackened chicken breasts, 71
blue cheese-chive pennies,
240
blueberries: blueberry-
hazelnut cheesecake,
248
Maryland peach and
blueberry pie, 42
Boston baked beans, 32
Boston brown bread, 36
Boston cream pie, 38
bread: Boston brown bread,
36
Charleston cheese corn
bread, 76
Navajo fry bread, 160
Shaker summer pudding, 40
spoonbread, 75
tomato sandwiches with
olive mayonnaise, 172
bread and butter pickles,
116
brethren's cider pie, 44
broccoli: fusilli with turkey,
tomatoes and broccoli,
193
brown sugar pie, 120
burritos: black bean burritos,
140

C

cabbage: baked pork loin
with red cabbage and
apples, 106
coleslaw, 34
Cajun "popcorn" with basil
mayonnaise, 57
cakes: banana lemon layer
cake, 83
black walnut layer cake, 124
Boston cream pie, 38
chocolate cinnamon cake
with banana sauce, 162
huckleberry coffee cake, 115
lemon pound cake, 210
Mississippi mud cake, 82
California taco salad with
beef, 182
California taco salad with
chicken, 182
Cape Cod fried clams, 16
caramel: caramel-baked
acorn squash, 110
flan, 168
carrots: mashed carrots and
parsnips, 110
pot-roasted veal chops with
carrots, 237
casseroles see stews and
casseroles
catfish: blackened catfish
fillets, 71
fried catfish fillets with
pipquant sauce, 63
cauliflower: cauliflower au
gratin, 238
celery: stuffed celery sticks,
96
Charleston cheese corn
bread, 76
cheddar and bacon biscuits,
112
cheese: blue cheese-chive
pennies, 240
cauliflower au gratin, 238
Charleston cheese corn
bread, 76
cheddar and bacon biscuits,
112
chiles rellenos, 138
dilled smoked salmon
spread, 240
fromajardis, 54
goat cheese salad, 178
herbed goat cheese dip, 204

huevos rancheros, 132
individual goat cheese
 tarts, 174
macaroni and blue cheese,
 217
Oregon blue cheese
 burgers, 234
stuffed celery sticks, 96
stuffed potato skins, 224
tomato-blue cheese soup
 with bacon, 216
Wisconsin cheddar and
 chive biscuits, 112
zucchini-cheese casserole,
 184
cheesecake: blueberry-
 hazelnut cheesecake,
 248
cherries: cherry compote, 122
Chesapeake melon and crab
 meat salad, 12
Chicago deep-pan pizza, 98
chicken: blackened chicken
 breasts, 71
California taco salad with
 chicken, 182
chicken Brunswick stew, 26
chicken with white wine,
 olives, and garlic, 194
chicken tacos, 146
chicken-mushroom pie, 232
dirty rice, 74
Galveston chicken, 144
lemon chicken with
 guacamole sauce, 190
oven "fried" chicken, 70
pan-fried honey chicken
 drumsticks, 100
San Francisco chicken
 wings, 185
tortilla soup, 130
chili: black bean chili, 141
clam and sausage chili, 227
vegetable chili, 95
chilies: chiles rellenos, 138
pork chops with chili-
 nectarine relish, 196
pork chops with sour green
 chili salsa, 148
tomato salsa, 156
see also jalapeños
chilled asparagus soup, 11
chives: blue cheese-chive
 pennies, 240
Wisconsin cheddar and
 chive biscuits, 112

chocolate: Boston cream pie,
 38
chocolate cinnamon cake
 with banana sauce, 162
chocolate, coconut and
 macadamia parfait, 208
chocolate-coffee-vanilla
 pudding cups 250
Mississippi mud cake, 82
toffee bars, 126
winter warmer, 242
chorizo: turkey-chorizo tacos,
 146
chowders see soups and
 chowders
chutney: fresh pineapple-
 mint chutney, 201
cider: brethren's cider pie, 44
pork chops with cider and
 apples, 230
cioppino, 188
clams: Cape Cod fried clams,
 16
clam and sausage chili, 227
New England clam
 chowder, 10
spaghetti with clams, 23
coconut: chocolate, coconut
 and macadamia parfait,
 208
piña colada fruit salad, 210
Southern ambrosia, 84
coffee: chocolate-coffee-
 vanilla pudding cups 250
ham with red-eye gravy, 68
Idaho beef stew, 236
Mexican hot fudge
 sundaes, 164
Mississippi mud cake, 82
coffee cake: huckleberry
 coffee cake, 115
coleslaw, 34
collards and rice, 72
cookies: applesauce cookies,
 126
New Mexico Christmas
 biscochitos, 165
toffee bars, 126
corn: Charleston cheese corn
 bread, 76
chicken Brunswick stew, 26
corn maque choux, 72
corn oysters, 112
Maine broiled lobster
 dinner, 24
shrimp and corn bisque, 51

turkey breasts with tomato-
 corn salsa, 145
Cornish hens with raisin-
 walnut stuffing, 192
corned beef: red flannel hash
 with corned beef, 30
cornmeal: Charleston cheese
 corn bread, 76
cornmeal biscuits, 78
cornmeal-coated Gulf
 shrimp, 143
hush puppies, 76
lamb stew with cornmeal
 dumplings, 150
Philadelphia scrapple, 30
spoonbread, 75
tamale pie, 151
country meat loaf, 104
crab: Chesapeake melon and
 crab meat salad, 12
crab Bayou, 56
crab Louis, 176
crab soufflé, 25
Maryland crab cakes with
 tartar sauce, 18
Old Westbury flounder
 with crab, 20
seafood and sausage gumbo,
 64
cranberry ice, 46
crawfish: Cajun "popcorn"
 with basil mayonnaise,
 57
crawfish or shrimp etouffée,
 60
cucumber: bread and butter
 pickles, 116
custard: flan, 168
Vermont baked maple
 custard, 46

desert nachos, 132
dill: dilled smoked salmon
 spread, 240
dips: avocado dressing, 204
bean dip, 161
guacamole, 156
herbed goat cheese dip,
 204
dirty rice, 74
dressings: avocado dressing,
 204
dried fruit: Pueblo pastelitos,
 166

easy hazelnut fudge, 242
easy peanut butter fudge, 242
eggplant: beef and eggplant
 stir-fry with ginger, 198
eggplant ratatouille, 202
shrimp-stuffed eggplant, 58
eggs: eggs Benedict, 17
huevos rancheros, 132
pickled eggs and beets, 116
San Antonio tortilla, 135
stuffed deviled eggs, 96
enchilada sauce, 158
enchiladas: beef enchiladas,
 152

fajitas: pork fajitas, 149
fish: cioppino, 188
Seattle fish fritters, 220
see also catfish; flounder etc.
flan, 168
flounder: Old Westbury
 flounder with crab, 20
fresh pineapple-mint
 chutney, 201
French Quarter beignets, 79
fried catfish fillets with
 piquant sauce, 63
fried tomatoes with ham, 34
fromajardis, 54
fruit: berry salsa, 200
piña colada fruit salad, 210
Shaker summer pudding, 40
see also apples; bananas etc.
fudge: easy hazelnut fudge,
 242
easy peanut butter fudge,
 242
Mexican hot fudge
 sundaes, 164
fusilli with turkey, tomatoes
 and broccoli, 193

Galveston chicken, 144
garlicky sautéed zucchini, 202
gazpacho, 173
Georgia peanut butter pie, 80
ginger: beef and eggplant stir-
 fry with ginger, 198
spicy sauerbraten with
 gingersnap gravy, 108

goat cheese: goat cheese
salad, 178
herbed goat cheese dip,
204
individual goat cheese
tarts, 174
grapefruit: pink grapefruit
sherbet, 86
guacamole: guacamole, 156
lemon chicken with
guacamole sauce, 190
gumbo: seafood and sausage
gumbo, 64

H

ham: fried tomatoes with
ham, 34
ham with red-eye gravy, 68
pirozhki with ham filling, 99
Harvard beets, 32
hazelnuts: blueberry-hazelnut
cheesecake, 248
easy hazelnut fudge, 242
herbed goat cheese dip, 204
herbs: salmon with sizzling
herbs, 229
see also basil; chives etc.
horseradish: pan-fried trout
with horseradish sauce,
228
huckleberries: huckleberry
coffee cake, 115
Indian beef and berry soup,
92
huevos rancheros, 132
hush puppies, 76

I

ice cream: chocolate,
coconut, and macadamia
parfait, 208
Mexican hot fudge
sundaes, 164
Idaho beef stew, 236
Indian beef and berry soup, 92
individual goat cheese tarts,
174

J

jalapeños: Arizona jalapeño-
onion quiche, 134
berry salsa, 200
desert nachos, 132

K

kabobs: Long Island scallop
and mussel kabobs, 13
shrimp kabobs with plum
sauce, 189
key lime sherbet, 87
kiwi fruit: piña colada fruit
salad, 210

L

lamb: lamb stew with
cornmeal dumplings,
150
roast leg of lamb with
pesto, 197
leeks: chilled asparagus soup,
11
steak with mushrooms and
leeks in red wine, 235
lemons: banana lemon layer
cake, 83
lemon chicken with
guacamole sauce, 190
lemon pound cake, 210
lentils: smoked turkey and
lentil soup, 215
three-bean and lentil salad,
179
limes: key lime sherbet, 87
lobster: lobster soufflé, 25
Maine broiled lobster
dinner, 24
lone star steak and potato
dinner, 154
Long Island scallop and
mussel kabobs, 13

M

macadamia nuts: chocolate,
coconut and macadamia
parfait, 208
macaroni and blue cheese, 217
maple syrup: apple maple
dumplings, 121
brethren's cider pie, 44
Vermont baked maple
custard, 46
Maryland crab cakes with
tartar sauce, 18
Maryland peach and
blueberry pie, 42
mashed carrots and parsnips,
110

mayonnaise: Cajun
"popcorn" with basil
mayonnaise, 57
tomato sandwiches with
olive mayonnaise, 172
meat see bacon; beef etc.
meat loaf: country meat loaf,
104
turkey meat loaf, 194
melon: Chesapeake melon
and crab meat salad, 12
Mexican hot fudge sundaes,
164
Miami chilled avocado soup,
50
Milwaukee onion shortcake,
114
mint: fresh pineapple-mint
chutney, 201
Mississippi mud cake, 82
mushrooms: chicken-
mushroom pie, 232
steak with mushrooms and
leeks in red wine, 235
mussels: cioppino, 188
Long Island scallop and
mussel kabobs, 13
Penn Cove steamed
mussels, 223

N

nachos: desert nachos, 132
Navajo fry bread, 160
nectarines: pork chops with
chili-nectarine relish,
196
New England clam chowder,
10
New Mexico Christmas
biscochitos, 165
Northwestern brown betty,
244
nuts see hazelnuts;
macadamia nuts etc.

O

oatmeal pan-fried trout, 100
Old Westbury flounder with
crab, 20
olives: chicken with white
wine, olives, and garlic,
194
tomato sandwiches with
olive mayonnaise, 172

onions: Arizona jalapeño-
onion quiche, 134
bread and butter pickles,
116
Milwaukee onion
shortcake, 114
onion rivel soup, 90
oranges: orange sherbet, 86
Southern ambrosia, 84
tangerine-soy marinated
salmon, 187
Oregon blue cheese burgers,
234
oven "fried" chicken, 70
oysters: oyster stew, 14
oysters Rockefeller, 14
scalloped oysters, 222

P

Palm Beach papaya and
avocado salad, 52
pan-fried honey chicken
drumsticks, 100
pan-fried trout with
horseradish sauce, 228
papaya: Palm Beach papaya
and avocado salad, 52
parsnips: mashed carrots and
parsnips, 110
pasta: artichoke pasta salad,
180
fusilli with turkey, tomatoes
and broccoli, 193
macaroni and blue cheese,
217
pasta with scallops, 226
pasta with zucchini sauce,
202
smoked trout pasta salad,
218
peaches: baked peaches with
raspberry sauce, 207
Maryland peach and
blueberry pie, 42
peanut butter: easy peanut
butter fudge, 242
Georgia peanut butter pie,
80
pears: Northwestern brown
betty, 244
zinfandel poached pears, 206
pecans: pecan pralines, 84
pecan-stuffed pork chops, 68
Penn Cove steamed mussels,
223

Pennsylvania Dutch fried tomatoes, 34
pesto: roast leg of lamb with pesto, 197
Philadelphia scrapple, 30
pickles: bread and butter pickles, 116
pickled eggs and beets, 116
pies: brethren's cider pie, 44
brown sugar pie, 120
chicken-mushroom pie, 232
Georgia peanut butter pie, 80
Maryland peach and blueberry pie, 42
rhubarb pie, 118
piña colada fruit salad, 210
pineapple: fresh pineapple-mint chutney, 201
piña colada fruit salad, 210
Southern ambrosia, 84
pink grapefruit sherbet, 86
pinto bean salad, 137
pirozhki with ham filling, 99
pizza: Chicago deep-pan pizza, 98
turkey and avocado pita pizzas, 175
plums: shrimp kabobs with plum sauce, 189
poolside tuna salad, 176
pork: baked pork loin with red cabbage and apples, 106
country meat loaf, 104
dirty rice, 74
pecan-stuffed pork chops, 68
Philadelphia scrapple, 30
pork braised in beer, 231
pork chops with chili-nectarine relish, 196
pork chops with cider and apples, 230
pork chops with sour green chili salsa, 148
pork fajitas, 149
pork jambalaya, 67
spareribs with sauerkraut, 105
spicy New Mexico pork stew, 146
twin cities meatballs, 103
pot roast: pot-roasted veal chops with carrots, 237
yankee pot roast, 28
potatoes: bacon-stuffed potato skins, 224

lone star steak and potato dinner, 154
San Antonio tortilla, 135
stuffed potato skins, 224
pralines: pecan pralines, 84
puddings: chocolate-coffee-vanilla pudding cups, 250
Shaker summer pudding, 40
Southwestern rice pudding, 169
pueblo pastelitos, 166
pumpkin: spiced pumpkin soup, 92

Q

quiche: Arizona jalapeño-onion quiche, 134

R

rabbit: smothered rabbit, 66
raspberries: asparagus with creamy raspberry vinaigrette, 181
baked peaches with raspberry sauce, 207
red cabbage: baked pork loin with red cabbage and apples, 106
red flannel hash with corned beef, 30
red snapper: red snapper with cilantro salsa, 142
relish: pork chops with chili-nectarine relish, 196
swordfish with bell pepper-orange relish, 186
rhubarb: rhubarb pie, 118
rice: collards and rice, 72
dirty rice, 74
Southwestern rice pudding, 169
tomato rice, 158
wild rice pilaf, 239
roast leg of lamb with pesto, 197

S

salad: artichoke pasta salad, 180
California taco salad with beef, 182
California taco salad with chicken, 182

Chesapeake melon and crab meat salad, 12
goat cheese salad, 178
Palm Beach papaya and avocado salad, 52
pinto bean salad, 137
poolside tuna salad, 176
Santa Fe shrimp salad, 136
smoked trout pasta salad, 218
three-bean and lentil salad, 179
warm salad of black-eyed peas, 53
salmon: dilled smoked salmon spread, 240
salmon chowder, 214
salmon with sizzling herbs, 229
Seattle fish fritters, 220
Seattle salmon fritters, 220
tangerine-soy marinated salmon, 187
salsa: berry salsa, 200
pork chops with sour green chili salsa, 148
red snapper with cilantro salsa, 142
tomato salsa, 156
turkey breasts with tomato-corn salsa, 145
San Antonio tortilla, 135
sandwiches: Oregon blue cheese burgers, 234
tomato sandwiches with olive mayonnaise, 172
San Francisco chicken wings, 185
Santa Fe shrimp salad, 136
sauerkraut: spareribs with sauerkraut, 105
sausage: clam and sausage chili, 227
sausage gravy on biscuits, 102
seafood and sausage gumbo, 64
scalloped oysters, 222
scallops: Long Island scallop and mussel kabobs, 13
pasta with scallops, 226
scallops thermidor, 22
scrod: baked scrod, 20
seafood: seafood and sausage gumbo, 64
see also crab; crawfish etc.

Seattle fish fritters, 220
Seattle salmon fritters, 220
Shaker summer pudding, 40
sherbet: cranberry ice, 46
key lime sherbet, 87
orange sherbet, 86
pink grapefruit sherbet, 86
shrimp: Cajun "popcorn" with basil mayonnaise, 57
cornmeal-coated Gulf shrimp, 143
crawfish or shrimp etouffée, 60
Santa Fe shrimp salad, 136
seafood and sausage gumbo, 64
Seattle fish fritters, 220
shrimp and corn bisque, 51
shrimp Creole, 62
shrimp kabobs with plum sauce, 189
shrimp soufflé, 25
shrimp-stuffed eggplant, 58
smoked salmon: dilled smoked salmon spread, 240
smoked trout pasta salad, 218
smoked turkey and lentil soup, 215
smothered rabbit, 66
soups and chowders: chilled asparagus soup, 11
cioppino, 188
gazpacho, 173
Miami chilled avocado soup, 50
New England clam chowder, 10
onion rivel soup, 90
oyster stew, 14
salmon chowder, 214
shrimp and corn bisque, 51
smoked turkey and lentil soup, 215
spiced pumpkin soup, 92
spicy bean soup, 131
split pea soup, 91
tomato-blue cheese soup with bacon, 216
tortilla soup, 130
Southern ambrosia, 84
spaghetti with clams, 23
spareribs with sauerkraut, 105
spicy bean soup, 131
spicy New Mexico pork stew, 146

spicy sauerbraten with gingersnap gravy, 108
split peas: split pea soup, 91
spoonbread, 75
squid: cioppino, 188
steak: lone star steak and potato dinner, 154
steak with mushrooms and leeks in red wine, 235
stews and casseroles: chicken Brunswick stew, 26
Idaho beef stew, 236
lamb stew with cornmeal dumplings, 150
oyster stew, 14
spicy New Mexico pork stew, 146
zucchini-cheese casserole, 184
strawberries: berry salsa, 200
piña colada fruit salad, 210
rhubarb-strawberry crisp, 245
stuffed celery sticks, 96
stuffed deviled eggs, 96
stuffed potato skins, 224
sweet potato biscuits, 37
swordfish with bell pepper-orange relish, 186

T

tacos: chicken tacos, 146
turkey-chorizo tacos, 146
tamale pie, 151

tangerine-soy marinated salmon, 187
tarts, individual goat cheese, 174
three-bean and lentil salad, 179
toffee bars, 126
tomatoes: enchilada sauce, 158
fried tomatoes with ham, 34
fusilli with turkey, tomatoes and broccoli, 193
Pennsylvania Dutch fried tomatoes, 34
stuffed cherry tomatoes, 96
tomato-blue cheese soup with bacon, 216
tomato rice, 158
tomato salsa, 156
tomato sandwiches with olive mayonnaise, 172
turkey breasts with tomato-corn salsa, 145
tortilla chips: bean dip, 161
California taco salad with beef, 182
California taco salad with chicken, 182
desert nachos, 132
tortillas: beef enchiladas, 152
pork fajitas, 149
San Antonio tortilla, 135
tortilla soup, 130
trout: oatmeal pan-fried trout, 100

pan-fried trout with horseradish sauce, 228
smoked trout pasta salad, 218
trout and bacon hash, 219
tuna: poolside tuna salad, 176
turkey: fusilli with turkey, tomatoes and broccoli, 193
smoked turkey and lentil soup, 215
turkey and avocado pita pizzas, 175
turkey breasts with tomato-corn salsa, 145
turkey-chorizo tacos, 146
turkey meat loaf, 194
twin cities meatballs, 103

V

vanilla: chocolate-coffee-vanilla pudding cups 250
veal: country meat loaf, 104
pot-roasted veal chops with carrots, 237
twin cities meatballs, 103
vegetables: gazpacho, 173
tortilla soup, 130
vegetable chili, 95
see also acorn squash; asparagus etc.
venison: spicy sauerbraten with gingersnap gravy, 108

W

walnuts: black walnut layer cake, 124
Cornish hens with raisin-walnut stuffing, 192
warm salad of black-eyed peas, 53
wild rice pilaf, 239
wine: chicken with white wine, olives, and garlic, 194
steak with mushrooms and leeks in red wine, 235
zinfandel poached pears, 206
winter warmer (hot white chocolate), 242
Wisconsin cheddar and chive biscuits, 112

Y

yankee pot roast, 28

Z

zinfandel poached pears, 206
zucchini: garlicky sautéed zucchini, 202
pasta with zucchini sauce, 202
zucchini-cheese casserole, 184

NOTES

NOTES

NOTES

NOTES

NOTES

Notes